18/14

£2 -
geí

MANAGER REVOLUTION !

MANAGER REVOLUTION!

A Guide to Survival
In Today's Changing Workplace

Yoshio Hatakeyama

President, Japan Management Association

Preface by Norman Bodek
President, Productivity, Inc.

Productivity Press

Cambridge, Massachusetts and Norwalk, Connecticut

Productivity Press
P.O. Box 3007
Cambridge, MA 02140
U.S.A.
telephone: (617) 497-5146
telefax: (617) 868-3524

Library of Congress Catalog Card Number: 84-61000
ISBN: 0-915299-10-0

Translated by Nihon Services Corporation, New York City
Printed and bound by Arcata/Halliday
Printed in the United States of America

89 90 91 5 4 3

CONTENTS

Preface *Norman Bodek* xv

Foreword xvii

Part One **THE FUNDAMENTALS OF MANAGING** 1

Chapter 1 **The Manager** 2

One Position, One Accomplishment 2

A Clear Understanding of the Self
Autonomy and Unity
Influencing Superiors, Colleagues, and
Those Outside the Company
Evaluation Based on Results
Making a Real Contribution

Division of Labor Between Predecessors
and Successors 8

Permanent Assets
The Bequests of Your Predecessor
Three Tasks
Forget about Evaluations
The Problems of Those Who Evaluate

Summary of Chapter 1   15

Chapter 2   **The Two Aspects of Managing**   17

Introduction   17

The Occupational Aspect   18

    Maintenance Management and
    Structural Innovation
    The Four Stages of the Occupational
    Aspect

The Human Aspect   20

    The Manager's Responsibility for the
    Lives of His Workers
    Humility
    Trust, Motivation, and Development
    The Three Levels of the Human Aspect

The Balance Between the Work and
the Workers   24

    A Human Being Is Not a Tool
    Management

Summary of Chapter 2   26

Part Two   **THE OCCUPATIONAL ASPECT
OF MANAGING**   29

Chapter 3   **Maintenance Management**   30

Moving Into a New Position   30

    An Opportunity for Self-Development
    Three Points to Consider When Moving
    Into a New Position
    Mapping Out Objectives for the New
    Assignment
    Putting Internal Systems in Order
    Daily Management

Personnel Selection   34

Selection by Seniority
Selection by Ability
Selection by Experience
Selection by Personality
Selection as Education
Selection by Desire
A Comprehensive Analysis

The Work Environment   42

Partner-Oriented Division of
Responsibilities
Room for Growth
Building the Work Environment
Preconditions for the Work Environment
Obstacles Within the Section or Department
Insufficient Ability
Support and Dependence

Communication   52

The Cycle of Instructions, Execution,
and Reporting
Speeding Up Negative Reports
Preventing the Breakdown of
Communications
Transmission Speed
Transmission Content

Summary of Chapter 3   57

Chapter 4   **Structural Innovation**   59

The Meaning and Character of Structural Innovation   59

The Meaning of Structural Innovation
The Background of Structural Innovation
Absorbing Cost Increases

Types of Structural Innovation
Prerequisites of Structural Innovation
Four Difficulties for the Manager to
Overcome
Effecting Structural Innovation

Investigation   71

Expectations
What's the Problem?
Types of Problems
Standards for Evaluating Problems

Decision Making   80

Intuition-and-Modification Planning
The Typical Order of Decision Making
Start with the Problem
Examining Multiple Alternatives
Extracting the Lesson Within
Studying Management Technique
A Comprehensive Judgment

Persuasion   93

The Four Elements of Persuasion
Long-Standing Trust
A Strong Will
Analyzing the Other Party
The Agreement Process
Priming Others and Setting the Scene
for Change

Implementation and Evaluation   100

Implementation Planning
Model Runs and Education
Evaluation and the Future

Summary of Chapter 4   102

Part Three   **THE HUMAN ASPECT
                     OF MANAGING**   105

Chapter 5   **Trust**   106

The Manager's Character   106

Selfish or Selfless?
Enthusiasm for Work
Fairness and the Distinction Between Company
and Personal Matters

The Manager's Influence within His
Organization   109

The Ability to Influence Higher
Management
Views and Beliefs

Thorough Backup   109

Chapter 6   **Motivation**   111

The Meaning and Nature of Motivation   111

Influencing the Workers
Bringing Out the Buried Will to Work
Removing Individual Obstacles

The Prerequisites for Motivation   114

Correct Your Own Bad Habits
Dealing with Negative Factors Within
the Organization

Motivating Individuals   117

Recognize Each Individual's Strongest
Points
How to Make Work Interesting
Dealing with Problem Workers
When a Worker is Discontented with
His Position
The Joy of Achievement

Group Motivation   123

Setting Attractive Group Objectives
Dividing Work for a Feeling of Accomplishment

Supporting Small Group Activity
Getting Away from the Role of Judge

Summary of Chapter 6　　　　　　129

Chapter 7　　**Development**　　　　　131

The Meaning and Nature of Development　　131

Changing the Workers
The Objective of Development
Believe in the Workers' Potential
Managerial Agriculture
New Challenges
The Manager as an Example
Work as Development
Work as an Educational Medium
Patience and Perseverance

Developing New Employees　　　　141

Developing by "Show-and-Tell"
Learning How to Enjoy Work
Basic Training

Developing Experienced Workers　　　145

Remedial Education
Three Things to Keep in Mind
Development by Entrusting
Entrusting and Timing

Developing Key Persons and Managers　　150

Training for Management
Guiding with Objectives
Workload Adjustment
Development of Managers by General Managers

Summary of Chapter 7　　　　　　154

Conclusion　　**Manager, Revolutionize Thyself !**　　157

Believe in Change
An Independent Development Program

Friends and Advisors
Self-Evaluation
Health

Appendix I   Managerial Growth Stage Checklist   163

How to Use the Managerial Growth
Stage Checklist

Appendix II   Manager Revolution Defined   167

Why There Are So Many Problems in
Noncorporate Organizations
The Crux of Japan's "Administrative Reform"
Taxes Are the Biggest Price Problem of All
Corporate Managers Beleaguered by
Maintenance Management

About the Author   173

Index   175

FIGURES

1. How the Results of a Manager's Efforts Show Through   13

2. The Four Stages of the Occupational Aspect
of Managing   20

3. The Three Levels of the Human Aspect of Managing   23

4. The Management Cycle   33

5. Vertical and Horizontal Division of Responsibilities   42

6. Ability of Staff and Support of Manager   45

7. Types of Structural Innovation   62

8. Varying Roles in Structural Innovation by
Management Level   69

9. The Process and Stages of Structural Innovation   72

10. Types of Problems   75

11. Costs of Problem Solving   77

12. The Order of Decision Making   82

13. Extracting the Lesson Within   87

14. Making Work Interesting   121

15. Horizontal and Vertical Division of Responsibilities   126

PREFACE

Why bother to read another book about Japanese management—especially one by a Japanese author?

A few years ago most American managers had no interest in Japanese management practices. There was a feeling that Japan was a nation of copycats without much to teach us. Also, Japanese culture was so radically different from ours. Their management behavior seemed to work only because of strict discipline and obedience to authority. And until 1980 the American economy was still the most successful one in the world. Most people felt there was no need to look elsewhere for advice on how we should run our businesses. But when the recession came and all of a sudden Detroit auto manufacturers were being clobbered by Japan, we finally started asking questions about Japanese management practices.

Something of "quality" was happening in Japan. And those of us who began to look and study found some very simple but powerful concepts. Quality control circles, participative management, Just-In-Time, *kanban* and flexible manufacturing systems quickly became known to most American managers.

Now, instead of ignoring Japan as we did just a few years ago, we realize that there is as much to learn from them as they learned from us. William Ouchi's *Theory Z*, Richard Schonberger's *Japanese Manufacturing Techniques*, Ryuji Fukuda's *Managerial Engineering*, Shigeo Shingo's *Study of the Toyota Production System*, and many other books on Japanese management are today being devoured voraciously by American managers. They attest to a new hunger for systems that work to create better organizations and better places for people to work.

In the past few years I have conducted several industrial study missions to Japan. On one of these I was introduced to *Manager Revolution!* Here was a book that seemed to cover in detail all of the basic fundamentals of the Japanese success story. But Yoshio Hatakeyama, the President of the Japan Management Association, whose books have sold millions of copies in Japan, was virtually unknown in this country. Why? Simply because none of his works were available in English.

After having this book translated, I found that the secret of Japan's success went beyond mystique and magic; it was simply very practical, analytical and progressive management. There was nothing here that couldn't be used in the United States. Hatakeyama's contribution transcends cultural bounds.

I am sure you will find the book easy to read but also very demanding. It is demanding in that it will require you to think and learn how to act like a manager. The manager of the past, who dominated his group by power, by the authority of his position, will no longer be able to survive in today's business world. The very real need for quality and productivity requires the modern manager not only to get the best from his subordinates, but also to assist and guide those in superior positions.

You will find *Manager Revolution!* to be your best route to success. The book is perfect for managerial study groups and should have as profound an effect on American management practices as it did in Japan.

I would like to take this opportunity to thank several people for their help in bringing this project to fruition: Noriko Hosoyamada, who first brought the book and its author to my attention; Nihon Services Corporation of New York City, for a careful and accurate translation; Kazuya Uchiyama of The Japan Management Association, for his unfailing helpfulness in various stages of the development of the project; Patricia Slote, for editorial and production management; Russ Funkhouser, for the book jacket design; Prentice Crosier, for the illustrations; Marie Kascus, for the index; and the entire staff at Productivity, Inc.

Norman Bodek
President
Productivity, Inc.

FOREWORD

I have written this book to make a suggestion.

I suggest that the managers of today's corporations, government agencies, hospitals, schools, unions, and other organizations need to take a fresh look at themselves and their surroundings. I suggest that they need to revolutionize their consciousness, their abilities, and themselves.

Social responsibilities pose many problems for today's managers. Too many, unfortunately, either fail to notice this fact or are content to bury themselves in their work and ignore it. In Appendix II of this book, "Manager Revolution Defined," I explain in detail the reasons why managers need to reform themselves. The content of this reform may be summarized as follows:

1. Many managers in large corporations still concern themselves exclusively with day-to-day upkeep and administration: very few ever manage to make a lasting achievement. Every manager should aim to become the kind of person who can initiate structural changes and who can move his superiors, the other departments in his company, and those outside his company.

2. Another weakness often seen in large organizations is the failure of the manager to exercise an appropriate influence on worker attitudes. Managers must renew their efforts and polish their abilities to correct the bad habits of workers and open their minds, to develop the workers and endow them with new skills over the years, and to make places for problem workers.

3. Conditions in smaller businesses and the newly developing service industries have not yet reached the state of the large corporations described above, but managers are often deficient in either basic knowledge or in the ability to put it to use. Such managers must go back to square one and develop themselves starting with the fundamentals.

4. Managers in public agencies have very specialized abilities; they tend to be weak as individuals and not to be cost-conscious. We need to examine the quality gap between public agencies and private concerns, which has been widening, particularly over the last forty years.

5. Aside from a select few, hospitals, schools, unions, and other groups still seem unaware of the importance of developing the abilities of their managers. It will be important to educate boards of directors and arouse their enthusiasm in this area.

Manager Revolution! begins with a return to the basics. I have first outlined the fundamentals of being a manager, then moved on to discuss various work and personal problems. I will be very pleased if this book is of some use to my readers.

Yoshio Hatakeyama
May 1981

Foreword to the English edition:

This book was originally written with only the Japanese manager in mind. You will therefore not find Western theories of management used as the framework for assessing managerial problems.

Nonetheless, I believe you will find this book useful. For one thing, you will learn something of the weaknesses of Japanese managers. That alone will allow you to glean some lessons which are unobtainable from your own experience. In addition, many important problems facing Japanese managers apply to managers everywhere. The solutions devised for Japanese business should be transferable elsewhere. Finally, a growing emphasis on the "human" aspect of work is shared by Japan and the Western countries, particularly the United States. The approach taken here is thus in keeping with the newest developments worldwide.

I hope the perspective offered here will broaden your own managerial horizons, and that you will find some benefit in it.

August, 1984

MANAGER REVOLUTION !

PART ONE

The Fundamentals of Managing

A manager, in the broad sense of the word, is a person who manages a staff. For the purposes of this book, however, I have limited my discussion to key management positions and those who occupy them.

Chapter 1

The Manager

ONE POSITION, ONE ACCOMPLISHMENT

A Clear Understanding of the Self

The most fundamental task for any manager is to develop a clear idea of who he is and what his position is, and to use that understanding to identify what the problems are and how to solve them.

In today's society, where technology, as well as the needs of both customers and workers are constantly changing, it has become exceedingly difficult for top administrators and board members to grasp directly the most serious problems in the different departments of their companies. The managers themselves must therefore identify the problems to be solved and come up with their own solutions. They must mobilize their staffs, colleagues, superiors, and those outside the company to bring about the desired results.

Needless to say, managers must work within the policies and directions of their companies, but the absence of a clearly discernible policy is no excuse for inaction. Today's manager investigates within his organization when confronted with an ill-defined problem; he decides for himself what he must do, and he acts on his own initiative from what he believes.

Today's large organizations are expanding in scale and spreading out geographically; their activities are growing more diversified and complex. As a result, it is increasingly difficult for top administrators to delegate tasks to their managers. The manager of today is

2

more than simply the person in charge of a section or department: his role is almost like that of the president of a separate company.

The very first thing a manager needs is a clear concept of who he is himself.

> *Mr. S. took the post of president in a company that was heavily in debt, and in a short time managed to bring the company back to its feet. To choose the people he could use, he interviewed each of the company's more than seventy managers for fifteen minutes to learn their thoughts on the contents of their jobs, the problems they faced, and the solutions they proposed.*
>
> *All those who spoke awkwardly or were difficult to understand, those who said their sections had no special problems or seemed unclear on the problems they had, those who overemphasized the problems in other managers' sections or presented too many problems, and those whose overall use of the interview period was inefficient, he summarily "failed." He "passed" only those who clearly expressed their ideas on the problems at hand and the steps they would take to solve them.*
>
> *Mr. S. reports that he passed eight people and promoted them to important positions. Interviewing them again in the same way, he authorized plans that he thought appropriate and succeeded in revitalizing the company in a short period of time.*

Autonomy and Unity

Legislators, governors, and mayors express in public their intentions to do certain things if elected. They battle with their opponents in the elections, and if they win, they try to fulfill their campaign promises. Their successes and failures are reflected in the subsequent elections.

Managers do not operate under this kind of system, but in the sense that they are responsible for guiding people, their jobs are essentially the same. Owners and top administrators of companies concern themselves not only with what must be done while they themselves are still active, but also with planning strategies for the future; the duties of section and department managers have the same character.

If a manager's function were merely to relay policy from above to his staff, there would be no sense in hiring someone with an education and career experience.

The manager should know more about his department than anyone else in the company. The best way to keep an organization functioning effectively is for the managers—who are best equipped to recognize problems—to solve those problems through their own initiatives.

To decide what he must do in his present position, a manager must consider both the demands of the entire organization and the problems to be solved within his own section. The manager must first grasp the overall situation of the organization, then recognize exactly what is demanded of him. He must also be familiar with any conditions outside the company that might affect his section or any problems that need to be solved.

From there, considering the needs of the section and the larger organization, the manager must take it upon himself to make and execute any decisions for which he is responsible. He cannot merely follow orders from above, nor can he simply act with the interests of his section in mind.

When all the managers in an organization perform in this fashion, its problems will be overcome and an integrated harmony will be born. Only when this harmony exists can the organization respond to a constantly changing environment; only then can the organization itself change, grow, and forge ahead.

This is what is meant by autonomy and unity, a concept indispensable for today's organizations. And only the managers of an organization can make it happen.

The essence of the manager is in his own autonomy. The manager shows his true worth when he acts according to what he believes and then accepts the results of his actions.

SELF-CHECK

(A self-check section is found at the end of most sections. You may find it useful to complete them as you read through the book.)

What is your "concept of self" in your present position? Check the description that best fits your present state of mind.

☐ I could clearly state all the problems I need to solve and all their solutions at a moment's notice.

☐ I could think about it and speak, but I'm not sure how specific I could be.

☐ I only recently took this position and am still thinking about the problem.

☐ It's been a long time since I took this position but I still can't say I have any really clear thoughts.

Influencing Superiors, Colleagues, and Those Outside the Company

The second function that all managers in corporations, public agencies, hospitals, schools, and other organizations have in common is to *mobilize people* and put their concepts into action.

A manager mobilizes his staff to make things happen. He always does a certain amount of work himself, but the work he performs directly is not central to the actual execution of his ideas. His principal purpose is to use the power of his workers, to help them realize their potential so objectives may be achieved. The manager should be expert at making his employees work hard.

But for a manager to achieve his objectives within an organization, mobilizing his workers is not enough. He has to mobilize his superiors, too. Only when he can express his ideas convincingly and win the active support of his superiors will his objectives reach fruition. At the same time, the manager must be able to talk with managers of other sections and enlist their cooperation—he must be able to organize those on his own level as well as those above and below him.

Similarly, managers must have the same ability with the people they deal with outside the company, such as customers, bankers, and suppliers. The ability to express what one believes and win the cooperation of others is indispensable for any manager, whether he works for a corporation, a hospital, or the government.

The manager, therefore, must be able to distribute his energies in a balanced way and mobilize not only his own workers, but also his superiors, his colleagues, and those outside his organization. This is why today's manager is more than simply a high-ranking agent of the company owner: it is as if his section were a company on its own, and he the president.

Long ago, there were managers who handled their staffs well

but could not deal with their superiors. This type of manager cannot survive today. Today's workers can see all too clearly just how much clout their bosses have in their relations with other sections and top management. When they discover that their boss lacks power within the organization, they tend to begrudge their own efforts. If a manager cannot deal with his superiors, his workers will lose respect for him as well, and his position in the organization will be jeopardized.

SELF-CHECK

☐ I have the ability to influence and mobilize not only my staff, but my superiors, my colleagues, and those outside the organization as well.

☐ I feel relatively confident about my staff, my superiors, and my colleagues, but not about those outside.

☐ I have difficulty influencing and mobilizing my superiors.

☐ I am not good at enlisting the cooperation of other sections or departments.

Evaluation Based on Results

Managers are judged solely on the basis of what they have actually done. No matter how knowledgeable a manager is, no matter how many people he may know or how glib and articulate he may be, if he does not have the power to perform, he is nothing.

The organizations of a society divide up the work to be done, each with its own objectives. Companies work to provide better products and services at lower prices; hospitals work to heal patients faster and at lower cost. All of these activities are, in one form or another, designed to create new products or situations.

Because managers play the central role in all these activities, it is only natural that they be judged on the basis of what they have actually done. Knowledge and information are very important, but they are really no more than the means used to bring about new situations.

The responsibilities of management require a person who can make the distinction between means and ends, as well as between the substantive and the nonsubstantive, and be careful not to confuse them.

Making a Real Contribution

From all we have seen thus far, we could define a manager as a person who has *ideas* himself and *mobilizes* those around him to *accomplish* something.

A manager holds many different positions during the course of his life. For some of them he has necessary experience, for others he may have none at all. He may hold positions of established importance that have traditionally been occupied by many different people over the years, or he may take newly created positions for which he himself must lay the ground rules. He may assume a position that makes him shine out over his peers, or he may be relegated to one that looks like a demotion.

As the manager moves from position to position, he constantly encounters new problems. Moreover, in any particular position, there is a vast difference between what was required of the incumbent ten years ago and what the current manager must do.

The manager assumes a position and looks around to see what must be done. He mobilizes his staff, superiors, and colleagues and, over the course of his assignment, puts his ideas into actions. Then he moves to a new position and repeats the process of forming ideas and mobilizing people to accomplish something.

The eternal theme of the manager's job is to make at least one significant and lasting contribution to his organization during his time in each position he holds. A section manager in a central government office might lay the groundwork to support a new policy; an office manager might turn a store that was doing poorly into a successful operation; a community leader might revitalize a section of his group that had become stagnant; a hospital administrator might revamp a system to make available in comprehensible form the figures involved in overall operations; a factory manager might solve a longstanding quality assurance problem.

It is important that a manager be able to look back over his career with the confidence that he did what he believed was necessary, rather than merely remembering how busy he was in all his various positions.

"One position, one accomplishment": the true test of a manager is how well he has realized this concept in each of his positions.

DIVISION OF LABOR BETWEEN PREDECESSORS AND SUCCESSORS

Permanent Assets

The branch manager of a municipal bank told this story:

Mr. O., who is now the executive director, was branch manager of this branch six promotions before me. When he was branch manager, he approached the managers of four major corporations which seemed at the time rather unstable. He convinced the ones who had not already decided on their major banking partner to go with us—it was a very unusual way to do business. Now all of these companies have gone public and use us as their major supplier of banking services. The reason we have such a good track record in this area is that the groundwork Mr. O. did back when he was branch manager is still paying off today.

We have already spoken of the "one position, one accomplishment" concept, but there is an important condition attached to the accomplishment: it must not simply vanish into thin air after the manager moves to another position. The accomplishment must continue to function after the manager who created it moves on to his next position; it must be a *permanent asset* that continues to contribute to the organization as time wears on.

When a manager moves to a new position, he is faced with two tasks: (1) carrying on the routine work of that position, and (2) changing the nature of the section or department. The importance of the first task is obvious, but the "one accomplishment" we have discussed refers to the second. Mr. O. made revolutionary changes in the composition of his branch's clientele, and this accomplishment is responsible for the branch's success even today.

It is very easy to carry on routine work and very hard to make substantial changes. Making changes requires much time and energy; the many obstacles to be overcome demand great wisdom. But ultimately, no matter how many different positions a manager holds over the years, if he does no more than simply carry on the routine work of his section, no proof will remain anywhere in the organization that he was ever alive.

The manager must work within the scope of his position to do what he believes in and accomplish something that will be a permanent asset to his organization. When he moves to a new position, he adds his own contribution to the assets left by his predecessor. In this way, the assets of each section or department of the organization grow continually, the overall level of the organization rises, and the organization continues to develop and win the trust of society at large.

SELF-CHECK

☐ I have made a contribution to my organization that could be considered a permanent asset.

☐ I feel that I have made a conscious effort, but I have my doubts as to whether or not it has resulted in a lasting contribution.

☐ I have managed the daily affairs of my position but have not made any lasting contribution.

The Bequests of Your Predecessor

Every manager must make a minimum of one lasting accomplishment for each position he holds. Unfortunately, the actual conditions that envelop managers are not as simple as this rule.

Mr. N., who had just taken the head position of the waterworks in a certain city, was shocked at the state of affairs there. He had worked for the waterworks in the past, but it had never been this bad: workers reported late, workplace discipline was poor, and minor incidents were inflated into major problems by the unions. Things had deteriorated so much that even the mayor was concerned.

The previous head of the waterworks was a man who enjoyed playing the politician: he ignored the internal affairs of the waterworks and then negotiated directly with the union leaders, paying no attention to the opinions and demands of the workers.

Unable to apply his experience from past positions to this problem, Mr. N. tried for three years to improve the situation. The board of directors suffered from a high turnover, and Mr.

N. eventually left his position with nothing but painful memories of his failure.

A manager is affected in many ways by the bequests of his predecessor. Many managers have had experiences similar to that of Mr. N. In such cases, where the new manager has inherited only negative bequests, the first thing he must do is apply himself unsparingly to resolve the situation.

In other cases, far-reaching plans were made in the predecessor's term that cannot be realized for many years. Some managers in this situation will reject or negate all that has been done earlier, simply because they want to do everything their own way. A truly seasoned manager, however, will evaluate the unfinished work of his predecessor with a calm and objective eye; if he finds it positive, he will start working immediately to finish it himself.

A manager occupies one space in one part of a larger organization that will continue to exist long after he is gone. No matter what state of affairs he inherits, he should refrain from making disparaging remarks about his predecessor and simply work quietly and diligently to solve the problems that exist according to what he believes. Even if he has something he wants to do himself, if his predecessor has left some unfinished task that is worthy of completion, he must overcome his reluctance and put all his energy into finishing it.

Working at one's own pace is fun and brings a feeling of accomplishment. It is frequently difficult for a manager to judge whether his inheritance is a positive or a negative one, so all he can do is act in accordance with what he believes.

"One position, one accomplishment" is a sound operating principle. Wanting to stand out, however, is not. Only a misguided manager ignores what his predecessor has left him and spends all his energy doing work that will make him look good. A great deal may be learned about a person from what he chooses to do first in his new position.

It is extremely important to carry on projects your predecessor has started for you. In some organizations managers fail to pass on to their successors records or memos of pending projects. In other organizations such documents are prepared and passed on, but merely as a formality; predecessor and successor may never actually meet to discuss the important points.

It is hard to see how such organizations can make transitions smoothly, so that the predecessor and successor effect a chronological division of labor.

Three Tasks

When a new manager takes over a position that has been well managed before, or when any unfinished work left for him can be easily completed, he can immediately take the initiative on projects he himself has chosen. This, needless to say, is the most desirable situation.

In such situations, the manager must make sure to retain the initiative he has taken. He must gather data and figures and learn the opinions of his staff and the desires of his superiors. He must weigh the entire situation of the organization, decide what there is to be done, win the approval of all involved, and strike while the iron is hot—that is, within his first three months in the new position.

Another obligation of every manager is to lay the strategic groundwork for his successors. Managers need to think about two kinds of problems: those that have already materialized and those that will lie dormant for years before surfacing. No problem solves itself: things only get worse with time, requiring the outlay of more and more effort and funds.

Laying strategic groundwork for one's successors entails spotting potential problems in their early stages and taking whatever action is necessary, either to begin solving them or to prepare for their eventual solution. In neither case will a manager see the results of these efforts during his own time on the job. Nevertheless it is the duty of every manager to effect a chronological division of labor—that is, to leave his successor an environment in which he can work efficiently. The fulfillment of this duty is the basis of the mutual trust and solidarity among all managers who take their responsibilities seriously.

Thus a manager must perform three tasks during his assignment:

1. He must finish what his predecessor left him.

2. He must take initiative on his own.

3. He must lay the strategic groundwork for his successor.

The degree to which a manager can handle these three tasks is a primary measure of his ability.

SELF-CHECK

In my last position:

☐ I had my hands full just keeping up with daily work and could not perform the three tasks.

☐ I finished everything my predecessor left for me, but could do nothing more.

☐ I finished everything my predecessor left for me and began to take initiative on some projects of my own, but was not able to complete these projects.

☐ I finished what was left for me, took initiative, and finished projects of my own, but was not able to lay strategic groundwork for my successor.

☐ I performed the three tasks.

Forget about Evaluations

It is extremely difficult to evaluate the job a manager is doing. In some cases a manager is forced to clean up a mess left by his predecessor; in others he may be able to sit back and receive praise when the efforts of his predecessor reach fruition—through none of his own doing. For better or worse, the actions of a manager's predecessor have a lasting influence in the organization, and the results of these actions are often hard to distinguish from those of the current manager.

A manager is unusually lucky if the situation he inherits is ordinary and average, and no manager can predict how well the strategic steps he has taken will be realized by the next manager. Frequently a manager overlooks a dormant problem, which then explodes in the face of his successor.

It is therefore very difficult to evaluate the performance of a manager accurately; in many cases, the prospects of having one's own contributions evaluated accurately are dim. What makes a manager a

Figure 1. How the Results of a Manager's Efforts Show Through

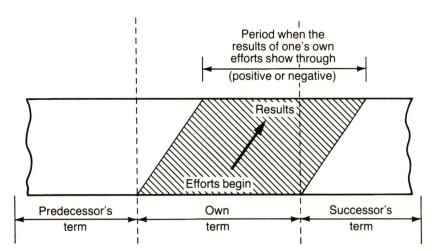

manager is the fact that he pays no attention at all to evaluations and simply keeps on living and acting in accordance with his beliefs, however harsh the trials he faces may be.

What this actually means to the individual involved depends on his attitudes and outlook on life; it is an issue whose interpretation belongs to the realm of individual freedom. But one thing that can be said for certain is that a manager's staff is constantly aware of just what kind of person he is, and their trust in him is determined by that awareness.

> *There is a conventional catch-phrase in the speech a Japanese manager makes when he leaves his old position: "I'd like to thank you all for helping me get through x years without committing any serious blunders . . ."*
>
> *Although the phrase is a standard part of any manager's farewell speech, it is inherently inconsistent, since whatever the manager leaves behind him does not become apparent until after his term has expired. It is mere presumption to use such words in a farewell speech.*
>
> *For a manager to say that he has passed a certain number of years without committing a blunder is almost like insinuating that neither he nor his staff has actually done anything at all. At any rate, "no serious blunders" is not good enough. You have to make some kind of significant and lasting achievement.*

The Problems of Those Who Evaluate

The people who evaluate, hire, and fire front-line managers—that is, company owners and operators, board members, presidents and vice-presidents—face many problems themselves.

These people must have a clear perception of the problems the managers have to solve. They must have lofty ideals, and they must help each manager improve himself and his abilities. The problems that each manager must solve vary widely from organization to organization. The only people who can grasp them all are the owners and operators, board members, and other top administrators.

In general, corporations conclude that if their profits are growing they have no management problems. Too much emphasis is placed on numbers, and not enough on how well managers motivate and educate their workers. Corporations do better in this respect than other types of organizations, but in general too little is expected of managers.

In government agencies, with a few rare exceptions, there are serious problems in the most fundamental labor-management relations. Workers have no real trust in their managers, and workers are discriminated against in placement and education depending on their status as either "career" or "noncareer." Too often, the research activity conducted is mere formality.

Small businesses and the newly developing service industries have not yet learned how to educate their managers. With a few exceptions, hospitals, schools, unions, and other groups are still further behind.

Throughout the world of companies and organizations, top administrators tend not to be fully aware of what their front-line managers are doing. Top managers must work to understand what is truly happening at least two steps down the ladder from their own positions: company owners and board members should be able to see at least down to the level of vice-presidents and section managers; presidents and vice-presidents down to the level of supervisors.

Such vision requires dedication and unusual ingenuity—a manager who is always trying to use the efforts of his workers to get a "free ride" is incapable of it. Established organizations tend to rely too much on personnel evaluation systems. The only way a manager can truly be judged is by how he performs with the three tasks—completing what his predecessor leaves unfinished, taking the initiative on his own, and laying the strategic groundwork for his successor—

and this is something no standard evaluation system can measure.

Today's advanced personnel departments place less and less emphasis on judging how each manager actually does his job. When this happens, accurate evaluation of employees according to ability becomes impossible. Such personnel departments and their advanced systems may in fact be more of a curse than a blessing.

The system of manager rotation is too uniform and automatic; the tendency is to neglect close examination of the managers. Managers should be rotated when they have fulfilled the principle of "one position, one accomplishment," but the time required for this varies between individuals. Thus, under the present system of manager rotation, some individuals are forced to stay too long in one position, while others go through their careers merely gliding along the surface of many different positions. Both results can present a serious obstacle to the development of a manager's abilities. Admittedly, this is a difficult problem, but I am still very dissatisfied with the existing attempts to solve it.

Not only are top-level administrators unable to evaluate front-line managers accurately, they lack the motivation to correct this deficiency. The proliferation of management evaluation methods that rely solely on the opinions of the manager's workers and superiors as well as the recent confusion about assessment methods provide glaring testimony to this fact.

SUMMARY OF CHAPTER 1

1. A manager is a person who has ideas himself and mobilizes those around him to accomplish something.

2. Today's manager is not merely an employee, but is more like the owner and operator of his section. He must have a clear grasp of the demands of his organization and the problems within his department, must convince those around him with the lucidity of his own ideas, and must act autonomously to realize those ideas.

3. A manager is a person who moves people—not only his staff and his workers, but his superiors, his colleagues, and those outside his company.

4. A manager is a person who makes things happen according to what he believes. The only way to judge a manager is by what he achieves, not by his knowledge or his experience. Never confuse the means and the ends!

5. "One position, one accomplishment." A manager must achieve at least one thing in each position he occupies: something that will live on after he leaves and become a permanent asset to his organization. Most accomplishments of this sort involve changing the nature of the department or section in some way.

6. The accomplishment each manager must make during his assignment consists of three tasks. First, he must complete any unfinished projects left by his predecessor. Second, he must take the initiative on his own and complete his own projects. Third, he must lay the strategic groundwork for his successor. The degree to which a manager handles these tasks indicates his ability and experience.

7. A manager should not concern himself with any evaluations being made of him. He should simply act on what he believes.

8. The top administrators whose job it is to evaluate and place managers must embrace lofty ideals, sharpen their abilities to judge, and rethink their methods of personnel placement.

Chapter 2

The Two Aspects of Managing

INTRODUCTION

The manager's job has two aspects: occupational and human.

So that he may help carry out the social function of the organization to which he belongs, the manager is given charge of one part of its overall sphere of activity. In a private corporation, the social function may be to offer superior products or services to the consumer for a lower price. Within such a corporation, the factory bears the responsibility for production, and the production manager helps carry out the organization's function by supervising the production activities there. Thus there is a logical sequence from the organization's overall social function through to the division of tasks within it, and finally to the responsibilities of its managers. This sequence is common to all organizations in society and is the basis of the occupational aspect of the manager's job.

The human aspect of the manager's job concerns the people with whom he is entrusted. Managers in any organization must work to win the trust of these people, to motivate them, to educate and nurture them, and to create a pleasant working environment for them.

THE OCCUPATIONAL ASPECT

Maintenance Management and Structural Innovation

The occupational aspect of the manager's job, regardless of the nature of his organization, may be further divided into two elements: maintenance management and structural innovation. Maintenance management refers to the stable continuation of the section or department's functions—in other words, the steady execution of routine work. In most cases, the organization has regulations and standard operating procedures. The manager sees that routine work is carried out according to these rules and makes appropriate decisions when any unusual situations arise.

Structural innovation, in contrast, refers to a manager's efforts to raise his section's productivity and the quality of its work by reforming the methods and concepts of the organization. While maintenance management oversees the execution of work in strict accordance with existing rules, structural innovation means that the manager actually defies those rules, reforming them into new rules, and imposing these new rules upon his workers.

Society undergoes constant change, and organizations must respond to new demands. If a corporation hopes to increase income levels for its workers and improve its product, it must confront new consumer demands as they arise. In the same way, a local governing body must be able to introduce new policy to respond to the changing needs of the community it governs.

Organizations differ in their constituencies, but none can gain the trust of society at large through a mere passive response to demands. They must therefore make careful studies of the groups they serve and reform themselves on the basis of their findings.

Everything changes, and change in today's society is especially rapid. Organizations and the managers who support them must respond to these changes, creating structural innovations in their sections both passively and actively.

The Four Stages of the Occupational Aspect

Maintenance management and structural innovation are fundamentally different in character. The former means operating correctly, in strict accordance with the rules, while the latter means the destruction of these rules and the establishment of a new order. Though these conflicting objectives are two sides of the same coin, it is no simple task for a manager to realize both.

Ultimately, however, a manager must be capable of both maintenance management and structural innovation, for both are required, without exception, in all the departments and sections of today's organizations and institutions.

The occupational aspect of the manager's job may be divided into four stages of growth. The first is *imperfect maintenance management*. In this stage, maintenance management has yet to be realized: the execution of routine work is hindered by various errors and difficulties. A corporation in this stage loses its customers to competitors and suffers declines in sales or performance. A governmental office in this stage earns an unfavorable reputation through various kinds of trouble with citizens. A hospital in this stage is overrun with errors and blunders.

This first stage is not uncommon early in the term of a newly appointed manager, but he should graduate from it within a year. If the stage of imperfect maintenance management continues for more than one year, the manager must be considered ill qualified.

In stage two, *maintenance management*, daily chores and routine work are carried out without difficulty. Errors and trouble do not occur, and operations progress steadily, but the manager has not yet become capable of structural innovation.

The third stage is *passive structural innovation*. The manager has graduated from the maintenance management stages and is now able to effect structural innovations in his department or section. He still acts passively, however, following directions and concepts given him by his superiors.

The fourth and most desirable stage is *active structural innovation*. Now the manager has learned to grasp concepts and directions for structural innovation on his own and act autonomously, influencing those around him to achieve these innovations. Graduation to this stage is the ultimate goal of every manager.

Three years' experience as a section manager should be sufficient to acquire the ability to make active structural innovations. This ability is one of the prerequisites for advancement to the positions of assistant general manager and general manager. Even when the ability has been attained, however, there are differing degrees of skill in application. The first step is to apply it to a single function of a single

Figure 2. The Four Stages of the Occupational Aspect of Managing

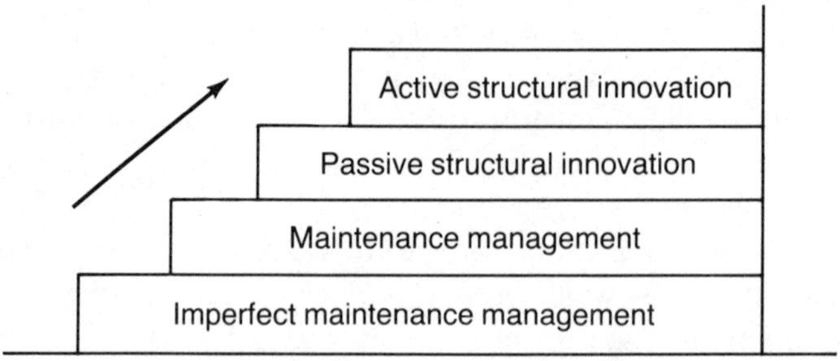

```
                              ┌──────────────────────────────┐
                         ↗    │  Active structural innovation │
                    ┌─────────┴──────────────────────────────┤
              /     │     Passive structural innovation       │
            /  ┌────┴─────────────────────────────────────────┤
          /    │        Maintenance management                │
       /  ┌────┴──────────────────────────────────────────────┤
         │      Imperfect maintenance management               │
         └─────────────────────────────────────────────────────┘
```

section. The next is to apply it throughout the section or department. The highest degree of skill in application is when a manager can bring about active structural innovation in a number of sections in the organization.

This ability to act autonomously, effecting active structural innovations throughout an organization, is one of the prerequisites for advancement to the positions of officer or director. This is true of all managers who wish to advance to executive positions.

SELF-CHECK

In the occupational aspect of my job, I am currently at the stage of:

☐ Imperfect maintenance management.

☐ Maintenance management.

☐ Passive structural innovation.

☐ Active structural innovation.

THE HUMAN ASPECT

The Manager's Responsibility for the Lives of His Workers

A very important issue in the human aspect of the manager's job is how his actions affect the lives of his workers. Consider the following example:

Some time ago, I went to certain company as a consultant and met a gentleman named Mr. S. He had graduated from Hitotsubashi and was the supervisor in charge of purchasing raw materials in the materials section. He worked hard, had a pleasant personality, and was well liked by those around him.

He lacked the arrogance often seen in competent young workers, always listening carefully to what anyone had to say. His skill in dealing with those outside the company was unusual for a man of his age, and he became effectively responsible for all negotiations with outside vendors and manufacturers.

Mr. S. devised a new system that not only covered the purchasing of raw materials, but included inventory control and unit control as well. He cooperated with warehouse and site personnel to set the system in motion and gained great respect for his potential as a manager. I remember no one else who had grown as much as Mr. S. in such a short time.

Later on I had reason to visit the same company, and I imagined I would find Mr. S. in a central management position. But to my surprise, Mr. S. had changed and seemed like a different person. The old gleam in his eyes was gone, and though he was already over forty, he was still only a section manager and was doing the same job as before. The man who had once been positive and aggressive was now dark and reticent.

According to the executives of the company, Mr. S. was a specialist in raw materials and was still a very valuable worker. Nonetheless, there was no doubt that he had lost his old spirit. Three times his name had come up when section managers were being reviewed for promotion, but each time he had been judged too much of a specialist, and not suited for a position in which he would have to deal with many different people.

Further, an executive in the personnel department said of Mr. S., "He's a very reliable guy, so the section managers in materials complained anytime we considered moving him to a different section. None of them wanted to have to do without him. Now it's too late—he's a veteran and he's become hardheaded. He can't stand it if things don't go exactly his way. The younger fellows don't even want to work with him."

Mr. S. had been ruined in ten years.

Humility

In the final analysis, the manager controls the lives of his workers. There are cases in which a worker grasps the key to success while working with his manager, and there are cases like that of Mr. S. It is no simple matter to predict how an individual will fare in a large organization.

Workers only live once, and they give their best years to their organization. Though managers work closely with their employees for long periods of time, cases like that of Mr. S. are all too common.

In Japan, managers usually serve longer than their workers; both their strengths and their weaknesses tend to be transmitted. The responsibilities a worker is given, the atmosphere in which he works, the human relations on the job—all these factors determine the worker's way of thinking and his future growth. And all are in turn determined by his manager.

Some would argue that a strong and positively directed worker will not be susceptible to negative influence from his manager. But those of us with management experience know well that a worker learns from and is deeply influenced by what he sees on the job.

The manager effectively controls the lives of others. It is essential for him to understand this fact and to face it with humility.

Trust, Motivation, and Development

The primary element of the human aspect of the manager's job is *trust:* the establishment of a relationship of mutual trust between manager and worker. Trust is the most important part of any human relationship, but it is especially so in the manager-worker relationship in which the life of the one is entrusted to the other.

This relationship of mutual trust does not arise spontaneously, but is realized only through the concerted effort of the manager. It may be a universal need, but it is very difficult to achieve.

The second element is *motivation*. The manager must arouse the workers' eagerness, so that the work itself becomes interesting and the workers become completely involved. The manager must make this happen for all the workers in his section—not only the men, but the women as well, and even the part-timers and temporaries. This requires special ingenuity and unflagging effort on the part of the manager.

The third element is *development*. The manager must develop his workers, he must teach new entrants their jobs and give them their basic training as employees, and later he must endow them with new abilities and concepts as they grow with their jobs.

Essentially, developing a person means first creating an environment in which he can grow and then giving him appropriate guidance. The actual methods vary according to the individual's stage of development. It should be the goal of every manager to help problem workers right themselves and become contributing members of the organization, to give everyone he works with both confidence and ability, and to make his section an environment that turns out promising and talented workers.

The Three Levels of the Human Aspect

The three elements of the human aspect of the manager's job—trust, motivation, and development—are interrelated as shown in Figure 3.

At the first level, the establishment of trust is the basic precondition for workers to feel motivated and give their best efforts to the job. If this basic precondition is not met, attempts to instill motivation in workers will fail. No worker will give his efforts to a manager who appears only to be using him as a tool for his own advancement.

Only when mutual trust is established will efforts to motivate workers begin to bear fruit. When this trust is established, however, the worker's job becomes so interesting that he involves himself in it completely. Then efforts develop the worker further.

Human beings change and develop during those periods when they lose themselves in their efforts and give their all to something. At such times the individual loses all consciousness of himself and does not realize until later that he has changed and grown. It is in

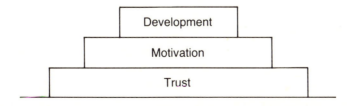

Figure 3. The Three Levels of the Human Aspect of Managing

these periods that we attack unfamiliar problems, breaking through the problems and gaining new confidence and new abilities.

When workers' involvement is incomplete, they blame their own failures on their co-workers or superiors, and personal development is hindered by excuses and justifications. If the development of abilities and concepts is to take place, each worker must feel complete involvement.

The manager must carefully analyze the human aspects of his section or department. He must find the correct approach to the problems that exist and work tenaciously to raise the level of his organization in an ordered fashion.

SELF-CHECK

Examining my section from the human aspect, I see that:

☐ Mutual trust is still insufficient and that I need to rebuild, starting from the very basics.

☐ There is a fair degree of mutual trust, but that my workers are still not highly motivated.

☐ I have graduated from the stages of mutual trust and motivation, but that my efforts to develop my workers are still insufficient.

☐ All three elements are fairly well covered. Now I need to continue raising my workers to higher and higher levels of ability.

THE BALANCE BETWEEN THE WORK AND THE WORKERS

A Human Being Is Not a Tool

Both the occupational and the human aspects of the manager's job have their independent objectives. The manager must see that both are attained and that a balance between the two is preserved.

People are more than tools. In the case of Mr. S. an experienced worker was, for reasons of convenience, forced to stay too long in one position. As a result, his potential was nipped in the bud and his talent was lost forever. Workers must not be viewed as mere expedients in the work process.

On the other hand, the egotistic mistake of overemphasizing people and sacrificing the quality of the work is equally impermissible. This kind of action will earn the mistrust of society.

The manager must find ways to allow the work and the workers to coexist—and there is always a way. The manager who refused to let Mr. S. be transferred was wrong. He should have let Mr. S. move to another section, giving him a chance to develop himself in a new position with which he was unfamiliar. He should have filled the gap that would have been left in his section through his own efforts, and worked hard to develop a new worker to succeed Mr. S. In this way, with a minimal expenditure of his own energy, he could have contributed to the personal development of both Mr. S. and his successor. Any manager who cannot take responsibility for the work of his section in the absence of a veteran worker is a failure.

Ultimately, the *occupational* aspect of the manager's job means working for the sake of those outside the organization by providing a better product at a lower price; the *human* aspect means providing an inspiring working environment for those inside the organization and raising the level of their abilities. The object of the manager's dedication in each case is different, but the two aspects are equally important, and the manager must make sure that they not only coexist, but actually influence and stimulate one another.

When the results of the occupational aspect are good, the confidence of the entire group is raised; the joy of accomplishment gives rise to feelings of trust and motivation. And when, through these positive results, the members of the group become more capable, the quality of the work performed rises once again.

Managers must understand this mechanism so they may lead their own workplace through a continuing cycle of growth.

In governmental offices, there seems to be a tacit division of responsibilities: department and higher-level managers deal with policy and work problems, while internal administration and human problems are relegated to supervisors.

This is reminiscent of the old military order, in which responsibilities were similarly divided between commissioned and noncommissioned officers. Were those at the higher levels ever actually able to deal with the human aspect of their jobs? In organizational management, the occupational aspect and the human aspect are two equal issues of exactly identical dimension.

Management

To manage means to control, or to make things move as one wishes. Management itself can be defined as that continuing effort which brings about the simultaneous and parallel realization of both the occupational aspect (i.e., doing a better job for a lower price) and the human aspect (i.e., raising the level of the workers' abilities and creating an inspiring work environment). A manager is a person who makes this continuing effort.

For this reason, a manager must first of all have a clear grasp of the social function of the organization to which he belongs, and he must act with a strong feeling of responsibility toward this function. For a corporation, the key function is to provide society with a superior product or service at a lower price—profit is merely a result of that function. Low-level, opportunistic thinking can lead a manager astray.

The manager must work to improve his abilities, so that with his strong sense of responsibility as a base, he may move from position to position, making significant accomplishments in both the occupational and human aspects of his role.

SUMMARY OF CHAPTER 2

1. The manager's job has two aspects: occupational and human.

2. The occupational aspect of the manager's job has two parts: maintenance management and structural innovation. The former refers to the precise execution of routine work, the latter to the realization of higher quality and productivity through the reform of existing concepts and methods. The manager must accomplish both.

3. The occupational aspect of the manager's job may be divided into four stages: imperfect maintenance management, maintenance management, passive structural innovation, and active structural

innovation. All managers must make it their goal to attain the fourth stage of active structural innovation.

4. The basis of the human aspect of the manager's job is the realization that, in effect, he controls the lives of his workers. The manager must reflect on this fact with humility, give his most scrupulous attention to his workers, and never lead them astray.

5. The foundation of the human aspect is trust: only with trust does it become possible to motivate workers. Only when the workers feel total involvement with their work will efforts to develop them have any effect. The manager must understand the three-layered mechanism of trust, motivation, and development, and develop strategies accordingly.

6. The manager pursues two ultimate objectives: to get the work done, and to stimulate the workers and enhance their abilities. Workers must not be used as mere expedients to get the work done, and it is equally impermissible to sacrifice work quality for the sake of the workers. The role of the manager is to lead his section into a cycle of growth in which the work and the workers not only coexist, but actually influence and stimulate one another.

PART TWO

The Occupational Aspect of Managing

The occupational aspect of managing is divided broadly into maintenance management and structural innovation. Maintenance management means the continuing execution of the section or department's functions. Structural innovation means the denial of this continuity and the reforming of the section or department.

Chapter 3

Maintenance Management

MOVING INTO A NEW POSITION

An Opportunity for Self-Development

When a manager takes a new position, it is important that he accept it positively and aggressively as an opportunity to develop himself and his abilities, and that he make an effort to use his new position toward this end.

Certainly he will encounter unfamiliar problems and new human relationships in his position, but it is an opportunity for him to grow—to gain self-confidence through new accomplishments and deepen his understanding of people. It is a chance for him to broaden the scope of his abilities.

Everyone hopes for opportunities to enhance his abilities, but such chances do not come very often. For a manager, a new position is the golden opportunity.

People generally approach their first managerial positions with great enthusiasm and work at full steam, but after they have held a number of such posts, the assumption of a new position becomes more routine. If the new assignment is in an area with which the manager is already familiar, he may react with indifference. But even jobs that we think we know may have changed both internally and externally, and the problems encountered today may be totally different from what they once were.

The worst thing to think is that you "know the job." It is essen-

30

tial to approach any new position as if you were totally inexperienced; you must discard any preconceived notions and approach the new position as a *tabula rasa*.

Three Points to Consider When Moving Into a New Position

I recommend careful consideration of the following three points when moving into a new position:

1. Your interpretation of your new responsibilities.

2. Obstacles you may encounter and things to be cautious of.

3. Your plan of action.

The first point refers to your deduction of what the organization will expect of you in your new position. Obviously it is impossible to understand the internal affairs of the section in advance and to anticipate every step you will need to take, but it is important to collect your thoughts on these subjects before assuming the new post.

The second point requires thought on what potential problems may exist in the position you are about to take, and what sort of attitude you should approach them with. In some cases, a manager who starts off on the wrong foot will have difficulty for the rest of his time in the job.

Of course there is no sense in trying to second-guess a new post, nor should one worry needlessly about the future. Excessive anxiety or caution is counterproductive, but a little caution will be very helpful when assuming a new position. Particular caution should be exercised when assuming a newly created position, or when the entire organization has gone through a major change. All too often we get ourselves into trouble by operating in the light of an after-image of how things used to be.

The third point involves considering setting forth, both publicly and privately, the steps you will take to overcome the obstacles you expect to find and specifying the order in which these steps will be taken. Doing the right things in the wrong order can lead to distressing situations, so a plan for action is essential—especially during hectic periods of change.

Any manager who is about to assume a new position should spend an evening carefully weighing these points and arranging his thoughts on them. The objective of the new post is, after all, to make a lasting accomplishment and to develop oneself, so a thorough and organized approach is particularly important.

Mapping Out Objectives for the New Position

After taking a new position, the manager should spend about three months familiarizing himself with all the work stations of his new section or department, and with all the new contacts he will maintain both inside and outside the organization. He should take this time to map out his objectives and explain them to all concerned. Hasty decisions based on presuppositions should be avoided.

The mapping out of these objectives has as its long-range goal the concept of "one position, one accomplishment." The three points outlined above should thus be carefully weighed with the years ahead in mind. More discussion of actual methods will follow in Chapter 4, "Structural Innovation," but as a general rule, methods should be chosen while the newly appointed manager is still "hot." If it is too difficult to arrive at long-term objectives, the manager should at the very least have short-term targets.

Putting Internal Systems in Order

Once the objectives for the new assignment are mapped out, the manager should closely examine the organization and systems of his section or department. This lays the groundwork for putting the section in good order to facilitate the achievement of the objectives.

The functions of today's organizations are in a state of flux. Internal structures and systems are often difficult to coordinate, and the people within them are constantly changing and growing. Managers should keep this in mind as they make improvements to facilitate the various actions they must take to achieve their objectives.

In examining systems, the manager must ascertain the degree to which work is standardized and reevaluate existing management standards.

Standards of work quantity and method are established as a way to maintain high quality and productivity. Because this standardization is at once the means by which new employees are trained and the yardstick by which work is supervised, it is the keystone of maintenance management. Managers must inspect existing documentation on standards and standardization and judge how well the policies have been implemented. If the implementation is inadequate, it must be corrected.

Management standards are the criteria by which the quality and results of an organization's activities are judged, as well as the yardstick against which overall productivity is measured. Management standards are necessary to allow the manager of each section to supervise his section's activities.

What are the criteria used in establishing management standards? Are they appropriate and sufficient as they are? Should they be simplified? Is a greater variety of criteria needed? The manager must consider these questions as he inspects past reports, makes changes in reporting procedures, and lays the foundation for his new assignment.

Daily Management

Once systems of maintenance management have been put in good order, proper management of daily tasks can begin.

The fundamentals of daily management form the management cycle of planning, implementation, confirmation, and action.

To bring about the desired conditions within the section or department, the manager must first draft plans. He then implements these plans, confirms the results, and takes necessary action. It is important that this process become cyclical, continuing into the next

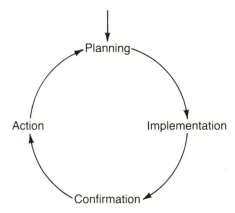

Figure 4. The Management Cycle

planning stage, but it is extremely difficult to impress the cycle upon every individual in a section or department until it becomes almost a conditioned response.

Too often managers act impulsively without proper planning, or their "plans" are merely drafted on paper and then neglected or ignored in the implementation stage. In other instances, confirmation is hasty or incomplete, or the difficulties discovered in the confirmation stage are skipped over and necessary corrective actions are never taken.

The manager must demonstrate the workings of the management cycle first through his own actions. By paying careful attention to each member of his staff and praising those who carry on the cycle in their own work, the manager helps all his workers internalize it.

PERSONNEL SELECTION

The selection of personnel is a key function of maintenance management: the manager observes the division of work among his workers and makes appropriate changes in each one's responsibilities; he finds suitable individuals to fill newly created positions; he makes recommendations for transfers and promotions.

Personnel selection is not only an element of the new manager's initial ordering of internal systems in his department, but also an important part of the ongoing daily management. There are six methods of personnel selection:

1. Selection by seniority.

2. Selection by ability.

3. Selection by experience.

4. Selection by personality.

5. Selection as education.

6. Selection by desire.

Selection by Seniority

When personnel selection is based on seniority, promotions are recommended and responsibilities meted out on the basis of the number of years employees have worked.

Although various criticisms have been leveled against this selection method, it has certain definite advantages. Perhaps most significantly, it usually evokes a minimum of negative response from other workers. In Japan, when a drastic or radical promotion is made without consideration to seniority, the chosen individual may be ostracized and lose the support of his peers; even if the negative response is not this extreme, the individual may take an aversion to his own success and give up midway, becoming unable to perform as he was originally expected to.

Even though the seniority method circumvents many of these difficulties, it is not entirely free of problems. The individual who is promoted often performs as well as expected. In many cases serious consideration is not given to the requirements for success in the work to be done, and the path of least resistance—i.e., the seniority method—is employed by default. The intentions are good and the selection method is certainly tolerable, but the promotion itself is a failure.

In summary, though the seniority method of personnel selection may not always consider the most meaningful criteria for promotion, it is a valid method for lower priority promotion and does not usually cause any serious damage.

It is also reasonable to employ the seniority method in cases where there are many acceptable candidates for a position, none of whom is much more competent than the others. In such cases, where the choice among candidates will have little effect on the successful execution of the work, the seniority method usually causes the least friction in workplace interpersonal relations.

Selection by Ability

At the opposite extreme from the seniority method, the ability method calls for a careful investigation of the abilities needed in a given position and the selection of the individual best qualified in those respects. Because this method assures the highest probability of success, it is a highly desirable selection method for today's organizations where immediate results are demanded, and should be employed as much as possible.

One flaw of the ability method is that older workers with a strong awareness of their seniority may become discouraged and lose interest in their work. There is also the danger that negative peer responses may keep the promoted individual from realizing his full potential. These difficulties can usually be handled, however, by a good manager.

Difficulties with older workers can be solved by skillful measures to alleviate their discontent; they must be taught to understand the changes that have occurred in workplace values. The difficulties that arise from negative peer responses depend largely on the maturity of the individuals in question, but the most important factor is the work done by the manager to make the promoted individual's job easier. Preventive measures and education are necessary to remove any obstacles that might harm the work environment.

Despite all the talk of promotion and personnel selection according to ability, this method is seldom followed consistently in practice. The problem lies in lazy managers who lack courage and the confidence that they can quell the negative responses of their workers. But a true manager does not simply leave such decisions to his staff in the interests of preserving "harmony." He struggles to allow teamwork and workplace performance to coexist.

Another problem with personnel selection by ability is that in many cases, the individual who seems to have the right talents for the job is filling another important position in the department. This problem occurs when overall worker education is insufficient, and demands further educational efforts on the part of the manager. In such cases, the more easily handled elements of the promotion candidate's present position should be passed on to other workers, enabling the candidate to continue carrying out the most difficult parts of his present position while handling the new position as well.

In essence, the greatest difficulties with the ability method of selection are encountered when there is too little trust between workers and management or when a manager lacks the ability to convince his workers to change their traditional workplace values.

This is undoubtedly a severely challenging method, but anyone who wishes to qualify as a manager today must exercise both ingenuity and effort to master the challenge.

Selection by Experience

The third method of personnel selection calls for the veteran worker, or the candidate with the most experience for the position.

In practice, most candidates are selected with this criterion in mind.

The advantage of the experience method is that the manager can simply entrust work to the individual in question and avoid a great deal of worry. Because a manager has so many responsibilities, a path that frees him from anxiety about even a few of them has an obvious attraction.

Unfortunately, this method has two major flaws. The first is that no one gives up faster than a veteran worker when faced with a new and difficult problem. Workers with long experience have great confidence in their work. They examine the problem, call on their experience, and decide on a course of action. This approach works very nicely when the problem is within the range of their experience, but when a ready solution does not present itself, the veteran worker often assumes that the problem cannot be solved. Managers who use the experience method of personnel selection should remember that veterans tend to give up when suddenly confronted with a difficult problem. The second (and equally serious) flaw of the experience method is that individuals with potential may be passed over and their talents nipped in the bud.

Most large organizations believe that these problems can be solved with personnel rotation. Nevertheless, the experience method of personnel selection is still too widely employed, maintaining "safety" at the expense of development. The major smaller businesses rely almost entirely on the experience method because of shortages of manpower. Some governmental offices favor rotation, but others keep their workers in the same jobs until they are virtually pickled. The development of human resources is a fundamental directive for all organizations, however, and simplistic short-term thinking must be replaced with careful consideration of the long term.

SELF-CHECK

☐ I have a tendency to keep my workers in positions they are experienced in, just to stay on the safe side.

☐ I do move my staff around a little, but not very much.

☐ I shift the responsibilities of my workers quite a bit and feel no anxiety in doing so.

Selection by Personality

The fourth method of personnel selection centers on the "personality" required by the job. Selections are made regardless of the candidate's experience.

Selection by personality is often used when there is an important job to be done, but many other sections or departments of the organization are involved and internal resistance to the job itself is great. In a case like this, it doesn't matter how experienced the person you choose is—if he doesn't have personality he can never succeed. A tough person with a lot of energy is called for, even if the position is totally unrelated to his own experience.

Similarly, for jobs that require long-term persistence and tedious repetition, a candidate may be selected because his personality is suited to such work. Or a man who is gentle and whom women can trust easily may be chosen for a position training woman workers.

The expression "the right man in the right place" means giving each worker the job best suited to his abilities, but personality is highly relevant as well. If each worker is given a job in which his personal qualities can shine through as he works, the probability of success will be high. This is the justification for the personality method of selection.

Selection by personality, however, is not without its weaknesses. A good personality for the job is not the same thing as the right experience. The major weakness of the personality method is that if it is continued for too long, the negative aspects of the workers' personalities will remain hidden and will incubate, until finally they spill out and cause the same kind of problems seen in the experience method.

Selection as Education

The fifth method of personnel selection centers on the education of the candidates under consideration.

The foremost responsibility of the manager is the development of his workers; he must try to take advantage of every available opportunity to enhance their abilities. Some of the best opportunities for this type of development present themselves when new jobs are assigned and when responsibilities are redistributed.

People acquire new abilities when they are forced to overcome unfamiliar problems. Selection as education considers what new challenges will teach the candidate the most: what kinds of assignments will best expand his abilities.

Workers who are talented and who can handle their jobs with ease should definitely be assigned to new positions that will demand more of their attention and efforts. If a worker is allowed to continue in a position that does not challenge him, he may become conceited at an early age and stop developing, or his excess energy may divert him from the path of success. Even if a worker does not handle his job with complete ease, once he seems to have mastered it he should be transferred to another position and forced to face an unfamiliar challenge. A work environment that does not operate in this way often leads to uninspired and apathetic workers.

When the worker's own education is the motivation for assigning him to a new position, his performance may slip in the early stages. It is therefore important to calculate how long the lag time will be before performance improves, that is, how much time the manager will be forced to spend on the maintenance management of routine work. Selection as education is, as a general rule, most effective as a means of promoting the long-term prosperity of the organization.

When this personnel selection method is employed, extra managerial effort is required in the form of guidance and backup, particularly during the transition period. For this reason, some managers dislike the method, but such self-centered attitudes will not lead to success.

Selection by Desire

The sixth selection method is to choose the worker who wants the job most.

The most important points in any method of personnel selection are first that the job itself be performed successfully, and second that the abilities of the worker who takes the job be enhanced. All other considerations are trivial. It is said that people do best at what they enjoy. Selection by desire is thus a simple solution to the problem of ensuring both the successful completion of the work and the development of the worker. Since it integrates the desires of both the individual and the organization, it seems an ideal method.

Unfortunately, because of their exposure to conventional personnel placement methods, most people have come to assume that the organization will assign them jobs. They do not go out looking for the jobs they want. We need to realize that this sort of dependence on their superiors tends to stifle worker involvement and inhibits the realization of worker potential throughout the organization.

Many workers aspire to a position for reasons that make good sense from the standpoint of their career plans, but fail to think about the order in which they should acquire experience, rushing all at once to fairly high-level posts that seem attractive to them. Managers should carefully explain to such workers the proper order in which they must develop. Workers who lack the ability to evaluate themselves must be guided, and all must understand that some jobs simply must be done, no matter how unpleasant.

The desire method of personnel selection should generally be given more weight with workers who have a highly developed sense of independence: researchers, engineers, editors, producers, etc. It is pointless to assign such workers tasks they do not enjoy, nor they will respond to prodding from their managers. The "specialists" have distinctive workplaces. Specialists in general have less regard for management; they dislike being tied down and show strong drive to work exclusively within their own fields. Whoever manages these people must take special care to see that individual demands do not clash with the overall needs of the organization; day-to-day communication must be maintained effectively, and unflagging effort must be made to develop the specialists' understanding of the overall needs of their organization.

SELF-CHECK

- ☐ I don't usually select a candidate for a position on the basis of his desire for that position.

- ☐ I sometimes employ selection by desire, but I still prefer the safety of the seniority and experience methods.

- ☐ I can say that I give sufficient consideration to worker desire and involvement in my personnel selection decisions.

A Comprehensive Analysis

We have examined as separate entities the six principles of personnel selection—seniority, ability, experience, personality, education, and desire—but actual personnel selection decisions are based on a harmonious integration of all six. We have also seen that effective personnel selection ensures both the successful completion of the work and the continued development of the individual.

Personnel selection decisions should be approached from two standpoints: that of the job to be done and that of the person who will do it. With this basic scheme in mind, the decision maker should consider the various factors in the decision, making a comprehensive analysis of all the possible disadvantages or dangers the decision entails. If the selection places a heavy emphasis on experience, the manager must consider the possibility of the worker's giving up in the face of an unfamiliar problem; if the selection goes completely against the order of seniority, the manager must consider the danger of the worker's being isolated and made unable to perform.

In some cases the dangers entailed by a proposed selection will be so great that the manager has to go back to the drawing board. In many other cases the manager will choose to accept the danger, and must then prepare himself to hold down the fort until the smoke clears. In yet other instances, the manager should analyze the decision from the point of view of its potential effect on the attitudes of the other workers.

Workers judge their organization partly through its personnel selection decisions, particularly its choice of key executives. It is important to remember that these judgments will be made, regardless of the conditions that prompt the decisions.

> *A supervisor in a certain factory was causing quite a stir. Those who worked with him showed great enthusiasm in their work; he was creating a new atmosphere in the workplace. Just at this point, the supervisor was transferred in response to the importunate request of the operations division, and a more conservative person was installed in his place. Despite the production manager's attempts to convince them otherwise, the workers interpreted the transfer as a sign that the company did not take kindly to originality and innovation, and they sank once again into stagnation. A number of promising workers left the company.*

THE WORK ENVIRONMENT

The next issue in maintenance management is creating a work environment in which people can best perform their jobs and realize their potentials. This task begins with the division of responsibilities between the manager and his staff.

Partner-Oriented Division of Responsibilities

The manager and the worker share the same objectives; they cooperate with one another to complete the work of the section. Each has his own role. When these roles are appropriately defined, the maximum amount of work is completed and the workers are developed. The manager is no better as a human being than the workers—he simply has a different role.

Human beings have different and uneven degrees of ability. An individual may be skilled in one thing and weak in another. The primary objective of the division of responsibilities is to adjust the responsibilities of one's partner to suit his strengths. Thus the division of responsibilities between worker and manager does not conform to any universally applicable law. In some cases the inability of one side must be supplemented by the efforts of the other, even if the job seems simple or unimportant. In other cases, even a very important job may be completely entrusted to someone who demonstrates a

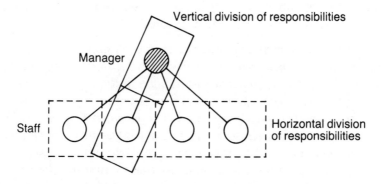

Figure 5. Vertical and Horizontal Division of Responsibilities

flair for it, regardless of his qualifications or experience.

If a worker is forced to attempt something he cannot do, the manager himself will ultimately not be able to fulfill his function and his staff will lose trust in him. By the same token, if the manager interferes in a job that the worker is perfectly capable of handling himself, the result is a waste of managerial time and a loss of worker productivity and development.

Ultimately, the manager himself must do anything his workers cannot do. Such things fall into two general classifications. First, there are things that only a manager can do, for example, making contact with and influencing higher management, enlisting the cooperation of the managers of other sections, or negotiating with those outside the company. (In Japanese society, a worker's title often determines his success in such negotiations.) Second, there are some tasks for which workers' actual abilities are inferior to those of their manager. These things can be done with direct assistance from the manager.

One typical situation in which workers come to mistrust their manager is when they feel he has made a show of being involved in a task he could simply have left to them, but has not actually taken any of the actions that might have made the task go faster—such as influencing higher management, enlisting the cooperation of other sections, or contributing to the solution of fundamental problems presented by the task. When workers feel this way they lose their desire to work.

This sort of situation sometimes occurs without the manager's awareness. In other cases the manager lacks sufficient vertical and horizontal influence and therefore turns his full energies back into his own section, where he merely gets in the way. This type of manager is unlikely to gain the trust of his staff, who may see him as "a lion at home and a mouse abroad."

SELF-CHECK

As far as the division of responsibilities between myself and my staff is concerned:

☐ Everything is divided well, and I don't see any danger of my losing their trust in the ways described.

☐ I have a tendency to interfere in things that my staff can already do while ignoring the things they can't.

☐ I'm not really sure how I'm doing.

Room for Growth

Suppose we have a job to do. The manager can do it alone and receive a score of 100, but if it is left to the staff they will get no more than a 70. One is reluctant to leave a job like this to the staff alone, yet it is also a mistake to say, "Only the manager can do it."

When I say that the manager must do whatever his workers cannot, I do not mean that he should do everything they cannot do as well as he can. In the example above, the staff should do the job to a score of 70 and the manager should fill in the remaining 30 points. If the manager tries to do every job that he can do better than his staff, he will die of exhaustion. Since the objective of the department is to become able to perform a larger amount of work as a group, the manager's key function is to fill in the chinks left by his staff.

Bear in mind that the abilities of the workers will be developed only when they tackle problems that are beyond them. To put it more precisely, if the staff can presently achieve only 70 points on a scale of 100, the manager should not simply fill in the remaining 30 points, but might, for example, provide about 20 points. He should fill in enough so that the efforts of the staff will just barely succeed.

When this is done, the workers are forced to stretch themselves. It is while they are struggling and contriving to get the job done that their abilities are developed. As they stretch, they naturally grow, and the next time they are confronted with a similar situation it will be within their range of ability. An experienced manager understands this principle, and guarantees the growth of his workers by skillfully controlling the ability gap between them and himself.

The first job the manager should do himself is that one job that no one wants to do. As a rule, the manager should take this job entirely upon himself.

There are all kinds of jobs like this—dealing with accidents, handling claims or complaints and apologizing to those outside the company, and taking care of emergencies—but no matter how clearly these seem to be the responsibility of the staff, the manager should, as a rule, take them upon himself.

Figure 6. Ability of Staff and Support of Manager

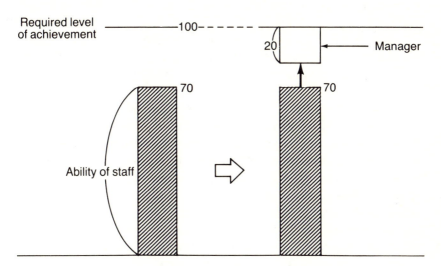

Working people in Japan suffer from latent feelings of persecution from their superiors. This can be seen anywhere when workers get together and go out drinking. Regardless of the type of organization to which they belong, the first thing they do is cavil and carp at all their bosses' faults.

This phenomenon has also been called a sign of their love for their organizations, but the message should be clear: the best way to lose the trust of your workers is to make them do those nasty jobs that no one wants to do.

Building the Work Environment

Building the work environment means undertaking activities designed to allow each worker to realize his full potential, specifically by (1) removing any obstacles that might make work more difficult, and (2) supporting the workers and supplementing their abilities so that work may be completed successfully.

The objective of all activities to build the work environment is to allow the workers to realize to the fullest their talents and potentials.

Human ability takes two forms: potential and realized. Realized ability is that which has already been demonstrated and is recognized by both the individual in question and those around him. Potential ability is that which has yet to be demonstrated—it is unknown to the individual and those around him, but it can be developed and transformed into a realized ability if an opportunity is presented.

The iceberg is a good metaphor for human ability. The visible tip of the iceberg represents realized abilities, while the invisible part represents the abilities that have yet to be realized. The invisible part of the iceberg is far, far larger than its tip.

Potential abilities become realized through the following process: the individual has an experience, succeeds, gains self-confidence, and his success is recognized by others. When a new employee enters an organization, the iceberg of his abilities is completely invisible— none of his potential is realized. As he repeats the process of trying and succeeding, more and more of his talents and potentials are realized.

Many factors, however, prevent us from passing smoothly through this process. If the work environment is too demanding, workers' abilities will not be demonstrated, and if a worker is assigned a very difficult task and receives no support, he may fail and lose his self-confidence altogether. A worker who has lost his confidence will not acquire new abilities.

The manager's prime objective in providing support and building an environment in which it is easy to work is to realize the potential abilities of his workers, thereby raising the overall quality of the work and developing the workers themselves. Backing up the staff's work efforts and covering for their weaknesses is an essential part of maintenance management. Failure in this will rob the workers of their will to work and earn their mistrust.

> *Mr. M., a general manager, was very good at making people work. His success was usually attributed to his experience in the operations division, where he managed the sales force.*
>
> *The moment he came to his position in the head office, the section seemed to come to life. It seemed that his new job was progressing well.*
>
> *One day he had a long conversation with one of the section managers under him. He spoke of a fresh plan that would require rearranging the company a bit but was eminently worth doing. The section manager began at once preparing for the reorganization, taking surveys, forming plans, and consulting with Mr. M.; he began working on the other departments that were also to be involved in the plan. Things progressed generally*

as expected, and the section manager, who was completely convinced the plan would work, continued his efforts inside and outside to prepare for the reorganization.

On the day of the meeting during which the actual decision was to be made by the executive director, Mr. M., the section manager, and the managers of the other related sections, Mr. M. suddenly had to leave town on urgent business. Leaving the apprehensive section manager with a few words of encouragement, he rushed out on his emergency day trip. The section manager tried his best at the meeting to convince the others of the validity of the plan, but the response was negative and the meeting ended ambiguously. The executive director was to go abroad the next day, and the final word was that nothing could be decided for at least another month.

The section manager, who had been working behind the scenes to arrange everything, was now in an embarrassing position. Because of the timing, all his efforts would have to be duplicated later, and he had lost face significantly both inside and outside the company. He consulted with Mr. M. when he returned, but there was nothing to be done. The section manager became the scapegoat for the entire mess, lost his reputation, and was ordered to take responsibility for setting things straight. During this time, Mr. M. became very busy with other work and left everything up to the section manager.

As a result, the workers' view of the general manager changed completely, and the entire section plunged into depression.

Preconditions for the Work Environment

There are four situations that demand managerial effort to improve the work environment. First, when the basic preconditions for work are not satisfied and it is difficult to perform work, the manager must remove whatever obstacles are present. A factory may have intolerable noise levels; the temperature may be too high; the lighting may be insufficient; or poor operational conditions may cause excessive fatigue and discontent. Similar situations can occur in an office. A sales department may find work inordinately difficult if necessary equipment is lacking.

Obviously these are all questions of degree, and will generally be resolved through common sense. It is desirable that the workplace be pleasant, but there are cost limits as well. In any case, the manager should be on the alert for discontent among the workers and be ready to take necessary actions before trouble breaks out.

As a rule, the manager should pay careful attention to the environment in which his staff works, taking necessary measures before complaints arise. His standard should be that workers have no grievances with working conditions. If grievances do arise, the manager must respond quickly and sensitively to each one, satisfying the workers by either solving the problems or explaining why they cannot be solved.

The second situation that demands managerial effort to improve the work environment arises when an obstacle originating in another section or department needs to be removed. In manufacturing, for example, if an early production step is done poorly, it may cause extra work and trouble for the workers in the later stages of production. In such cases, the manager of the section handling the later process must negotiate with the manager of the section that is turning out unsatisfactory work. Bringing the early process work up to standard will ease the workload at later stages.

The same kind of problem exists in administrative and clerical sections. If receipts are late in arriving at the accounting section or the computer section, thereby confusing section operations, the manager of that section must meet with those of the offending sections and get them to adhere to schedules. This kind of problem occurs regularly with the transmission of information. If the flow of information from one section is unsatisfactory and interferes with the operations of another, the situation must be rectified through negotiation.

If the workers in one section find that they cannot perform their jobs beyond a certain level because the workers in a related section feel differently about the job, the manager of the first section must meet with the manager of the second and reach an understanding so his workers can get on with their work. It often happens that the work of one section is made more difficult by factors originating in another section.

In such cases, the persuasive powers of the manager himself are at a premium. The manager of the other section will be sympathetic to him as a fellow manager, but he must also think of his responsibility to his own staff and the interests of his own section. Managers engaging in interdepartmental negotiations must therefore control their egos and make sure that they always act in the best interests of the organization as a whole.

There is a clear relation between the ability to influence others and the ability to build a good working environment. A manager who lacks persuasive power will have great difficulty improving the work environment of his section. This will be discussed in more detail in the next section.

SELF-CHECK

When I negotiate with other sections or departments:

☐ I work very hard and don't accomplish anything.

☐ I usually get what I want.

☐ I get varying results. I have relatively little difficulty with simple problems, but I can't seem to solve the more difficult long-standing problems.

Obstacles Within the Section or Department

Many of the obstacles a manager must clear away exist within his own section or department.

For example, if a worker cannot perform the job he has been assigned, he must enlist the cooperation of his colleagues, but if he is not skilled at getting others to cooperate with him, the manager himself must meet with the other members of the section, explain the importance of the job, and induce them to pitch in.

In some cases a worker knows what he must do, but feels awkward dealing with a certain other worker, or must work with a partner with whom he does not get along well. The job then takes on an unpleasant aspect. There are also times when a supervisor, foreman, or group leader becomes too immersed in his own job and does not offer the workers the support he should.

In sections where production is divided into earlier and later processes, the workers in the later stages of production may encounter unwarranted difficulties in their work, as in the interdepartmental situation just described. It often happens that a supervisor in some intermediate step gives poor instructions at the expense of the workers in the later stages of production.

If the manager has the right leadership qualities, he should be able to remove these intradepartmental obstacles readily. Some managers bumble through, turning their eyes away from the discomforts of their workers with only the vaguest notion of what is actually going on. This attitude is unacceptable. Such managers should be made aware how terrible it is to lose the trust of one's workers.

Insufficient Ability

Sometimes a job assigned to a group of workers exceeds their present abilities. A sales department, for example, may be unable to convince a certain purchaser to buy a product. In this case the support of the sales manager is called for. Or a section may be involved in some negotiations with an outside concern that are so difficult that they require the participation of the section manager.

The staff members may feel honored that their manager has entrusted them with an important assignment, but if they are not sure how to proceed with it, the manager must help them organize their thinking and give them hints on what steps might prove effective. The same kind of support is called for when a project runs aground or falls into stagnation and workers cannot find a way out.

In innumerable situations projects can go astray because of insufficient worker ability. Whenever this happens the manager must guide the workers and lead them, show them the way out of the maze, and if all else fails, get behind them and push.

No worker is absolutely perfect—and the same is true of managers. Thus there will inevitably be some jobs that the workers simply cannot handle alone. The duty of the manager is to add his abilities to the abilities of his workers and see each job through to completion.

When you entrust a worker with a job, it is important to forecast what will happen. He may rush blindly into things and fail completely, or he may be too slow in starting and never get the job done. The project may end in a complete standstill because of the worker's inability to negotiate with other sections.

There are many possibilities, but the outcome should be readily predictable when dealing with a worker whose character and performance on the job are already known. One of the most valuable skills a manager can develop is the ability to read his workers. The most important part of this ability is seeing where a worker is most likely to encounter frustration and where he is most likely to run into obstacles.

A manager must watch the progress of his section's work with a hawk's eye, and must always be on the lookout for a worker in trouble. He must never become so buried in his own work that he loses sight of his workers. Do not just play at being a manager!

SELF-CHECK

Have you ever failed to cover for the gaps in your workers' abilities?

☐ Yes.

☐ Never.

☐ I can't think of any specific examples right now, but it seems as if I may have.

Support and Dependence

The way to make workers approach their jobs with enthusiasm is to guarantee that they will never be left in the lurch when things go wrong—that the manager will always come in to save the day. The general manager Mr. M. failed because he passed on too much responsibility to those under him.

At the other extreme is the manager who, without giving his workers even a hint of the overall future plan, simply doles out minutely detailed orders that leave them no freedom to exercise their own powers of judgment. The workers will begin to harbor discontent and doubt. In the end, concluding that their manager does not trust them, they will lose their trust in him.

These two opposite types represent extremes, but every manager runs the risk of falling to one side or the other of the happy medium. A manager may tend to leave everything up to those under him without offering sufficient support, or he may be unable to entrust his staff with work and end up constricting them. Take a good look at yourself, and if you see yourself leaning too much to one side, make a conscious effort to swing the other way and strike a balance.

SELF-CHECK

☐ I tend to worry about the work my staff is doing, interfere too much, and offer excessive support.

☐ I do not interfere excessively, but I do need to re-evaluate the degree to which I help my staff.

☐ It depends on the worker, but I have usually managed to strike an appropriate balance.

COMMUNICATION

The most fundamental part of maintenance management is to ensure the proper flow of information both within the section and to the outside, and to maintain good communications.

It goes without saying that any information from above must be disseminated properly throughout the ranks of the organization. It is also important that reporting and contact inside and outside the section be tightly organized.

The Cycle of Instructions, Execution, and Reporting

Every manager must train his workers to report to him immediately on any action they have taken. When he gives them a job, they must give him the results before he asks.

The typical concept of work is that one person gives another a job to do, and that person does it. But the worker's responsibility has not ended until he has finished the job and completed the cycle—by reporting to the person from whom he received the original orders.

From the standpoint of this cycle, any manager who has to ask his workers for a report is not really managing. His section is bound to be plagued with mistakes and blunders. When a manager receives a report, he first checks it, and then looks it over to see if anything more needs to be done. In these few moments errors are prevented.

When a worker receives instructions, he must always report on whatever action he has taken—before he is asked. This is a basic requirement of work within an organization which must be impressed carefully on each worker in the first days of his employment.

If your workers do not measure up to this standard, speak to them and tell them that the report comes first, and that if they have to be asked, they have fouled up. Some workers may still require prompting. Ask them personally for their reports, and once they are delivered, warn the workers to be prompt next time. Repeat this process calmly until every worker reports to you automatically.

You, of course, must never need to be asked twice for something by someone under you. A manager must be a model to all his workers.

Speeding Up Negative Reports

In addition to reporting on tasks they were asked to perform, workers also need to transmit to the manager certain kinds of information they acquire.

There is usually no problem with reporting when the worker acquires information that is "good"—we sold more than the target, we solved a problem, we succeeded. This kind of report is always prompt.

The problem is with "bad" reports—there was an accident, we had trouble with a client, there was a complaint, a patient is angry, we're having problems with the residents, we failed. This kind of report has a natural tendency to get delayed. Psychologically, the worker responsible wishes to conceal his error, try to solve it himself, and then report it once it is solved. But the irony is that while there is no need to rush good reports, bad reports require immediate countermeasures, usually on the part of the manager. All too often the problem spreads out of control while the workers are trying various means to solve it. If their efforts fail, the problem may become even harder to solve, and the individuals in question may be accused of not being straightforward in their handling of the problem.

The manager must therefore impress it upon his workers that the worse a report is, the faster he must receive it. He must make sure they know that the surest way to turn a mistake into a fatal problem is to delay reporting it. This is particularly important for managers in today's world of rapid and unpredictable change.

Preventing the Breakdown of Communications

If a manager is impatient or overly emotional, communications are bound to break down. His workers will become sensitive to his moods and postpone making any negative reports on days when he seems to be in a bad humor. They will use very optimistic terms to describe something that is not necessarily positive, and on days when the manager is in a foul temper they will avoid him completely. In any of these situations, the manager will not receive sufficient or proper information and his judgments will be incorrect.

A manager cannot simply receive reports, smiling at the good ones and frowning at the bad ones—his job is more complex than that. Such responses indicate to the workers that their manager wants to hear only good reports and has no interest in hearing any others. In such cases it is the manager himself who delays the bad reports.

The manager should also guard against appearing overly busy. His workers may hesitate to approach him, and timely information or ideas may be sacrificed. However busy a manager actually is, he must take care to speak and act as if he is not. And certainly it is out of the question for the manager to run about acting busy if he is not!

When a manager receives no particular reports and finds himself unaware of the state of affairs in his section, he should approach his staff without hesitation and question them, offering any pertinent advice or support and making time to meet with them for discussion. The more contact a manager has with his staff, the better communication will be and the more freely his staff will approach him. It is very important for the manager to approach his workers frequently and openly.

When the manager and his staff confront and solve difficult problems together, the process creates a feeling of solidarity. The relationship between manager and staff becomes one of free and open communication. They go out for a drink together; they have coffee; they play golf together. Contact away from the workplace builds good communication. The manager's continued effort to become sensitive to his workers and build an intimate relationship without forcing himself on them is the key to preventing commmunications breakdown.

SELF-CHECK

Do your workers need to worry about your mood when they approach you?

☐ I guess they do.

☐ I wouldn't want to think that is the case, but I had better be careful about it.

☐ No, my workers feel free to approach me any time with any problem at all.

Transmission Speed

The biggest problem in communication is the speed with which it is effected.

In some organizations necessary information is transmitted promptly and correctly to the place it needs to go, but in others transmission speed is slow, information from outside the organization gets fouled up, and all sorts of internal problems are present between sections and departments. Generally speaking, organizations that have grown rapidly fall into confusion. When they were still small, one could easily see what was happening in other sections without making any special effort, and so little emphasis was put on proper communication. When the scale of an organization increases, communication quickly becomes much more important, but instead of making the necessary adjustments in their ways of working, people tend to just get irritated.

Communication is the most important job of everyone in the organization. Everyone must meet with others and hear them out. Everyone must attend meetings and learn what to transmit to others, and must take in information from outside the organization. Immediately upon receiving information, everyone must get into the habit of asking, "Who else needs to know this?" and transmitting the information instantly and precisely to those people.

A company that sold durable consumer goods decided to cut its purchasing costs drastically by ordering all its parts from one manufacturer it could trust, instead of dividing the orders among a number of different manufacturers, as it had been doing. While drawing up comparison charts on all the manufacturers' delivery records, defect ratios, and delivery lag times, the materials section conducted the following test under the orders of the executive director.

The materials section first telephoned the operations section of each manufacturer they had been patronizing, saying that they wanted to make some changes in the specifications of a part they had been buying and asking that someone call them to discuss the modifications. The people in the operations section at each company took the message and hung up the phone.

One hour later, the materials section called the engineering section of the supplier companies, saying, "Uh, yes, this is X company, we're calling about that part..." They then judged the manufacturers according to the reactions of their engineering sections to this call.

Most of the manufacturers responded, "What part?" They had no idea at all what the call was about, and so they failed the test.

Other suppliers had better internal communications. Companies whose engineering departments called within an hour to take the order for the changes in the part received a grade of A and were considered as candidates to become the exclusive supplier. Companies that did not call back within the hour, but whose engineering departments knew about the part change when contacted, were graded B. This group was to be judged on the basis of the other data.

I might mention in passing that in this particular field, the manufacturers have their operations offices in large cities like Tokyo, Osaka, and Nagoya, while the engineering sections are in the factories, in separate locations.

The problem is not simply how scrupulous the manager himself is in communication, but whether the entire section makes this a priority. Whether the workers are lazy or whether they are sufficiently aware of the importance of communication depends largely on the habits and abilities of the manager over them. If a manager is diligent in communication and transmits necessary information immediately to all concerned, his staff will pick up the habit.

Prompt, effective communication moves us and causes us to respond instantly. If workers receive information promptly and are still slow to transmit it, they must be admonished until the habit sticks.

Transmission Content

Communication must be more than fast. It must be accurate, concise, and easy to understand. Particular caution is demanded in the communication of items that contain subtle nuances. In matters such as hiring, compensation, and labor-management relations, a small slip in tone or phrasing can cause a big misunderstanding and a great deal of trouble. Or to give another example, if workers have to prepare quickly for major changes to be made in the organization, a major loss in trust may be suffered if the preparations are begun on the basis of preliminary information and the master plan is later altered.

In general, information should be transmitted to the workers as quickly and in as much detail as possible, to allow them the maximum freedom to judge and act independently. But the mode of expression and the actual amount of information given should be carefully weighed from the standpoint of the examples above. The manager must give prudent thought to how his message will be received.

We all tend to hear what we want to hear, to misinterpret nuances as meaning what we wish they had meant. The manager must therefore never mince words. If he means to say that something is no good, he must say clearly, "no good."

Some other important elements of maintenance management include proper handling of proposals, time management, conference guidance, and plan generation, among many others. These are technical problems and are therefore not considered in this book.

SUMMARY OF CHAPTER 3

1. When a manger assumes a new post, he must see it as a golden opportunity for self-development, and act vigorously and constructively. To ensure that he will be able to make a lasting accomplishment during his tenure, the manager must think carefully about

three things before he assumes the new post: first, his interpretation of what his new responsibilities will be; second, any possible obstacles he might encounter and things that may require caution; and third, his plan of action.

2. The manager must map out his objectives for the new term while he is still "hot." In order to achieve these objectives, he must put internal systems into good order and see that routine work is executed according to the management cycle.

3. There are six methods of personnel selection: selection by seniority, selection by ability, selection by experience, selection by personality, selection as education, and selection by desire. The manager must make a comprehensive analysis of each personnel selection situation, taking note of the merits and the dangers of each method, and then make the decision that will ensure both the successful completion of the job and the continued development of the worker selected.

4. Once the manager has made his personnel selection decisions, he must proceed to make it easier for his workers to do their jobs. He must build a good working environment by clearing away any obstacles that may exist in his own or other sections or departments, and he must supplement any deficiencies in his workers' abilities through his own efforts.

5. The manager must be careful not to give his staff too much work without providing adequate support, but he must also take care not to interfere excessively with their work and constrict them. He must evaluate himself and make a conscious effort to strike a balance.

6. The manager must create a workplace in which his workers automatically report to him before he asks. He must educate his workers as to the dangers of delaying negative reports. He must be especially cautious of any faults of his own that could bring about a breakdown in communications with his workers.

7. The speed with which information is transmitted is extremely important. The manager must train his workers to communicate all relevant received information accurately and instantly, and he must himself be a model to them.

Chapter 4

Structural Innovation

THE MEANING AND CHARACTER OF STRUCTURAL INNOVATION

The Meaning of Structural Innovation

Structural innovation means reforming both the concepts and the methods used in a section or department to attain higher levels of work quality and productivity.

Structural innovation as a fraction of management is very different from maintenance management. Whereas maintenance management means the execution of routine work in strict adherence to rules and regulations, structural innovation means reforming the rules themselves and adding a new dimension to the workplace. The manager is the central figure in structural innovation, which represents the fruition of the concept of "one position, one accomplishment." The manager must make structural innovation his goal from the moment he takes his new position, and he must take every opportunity presented him to effect structural innovation.

Structural innovation is nothing special or unusual. It takes place in every organization over time. The targets for innovation are myriad: the quality and cost of services, the conceptual climate among the workers, people, systems, methods, and so on.

There are many different forms of structural innovation. Some examples are:

1. Reforms in the workers of a division, or in the organization or prevailing ideas of a section;

2. Reforms due to the introduction of new equipment or facilities;

3. Changes in operating procedures;

4. Internal changes in the research systems of the operations planning, administrative, accounting, personnel, production, sales, or engineering departments of a company;

5. External changes, in the advertising, purchasing, or trading departments;

6. Reforms due to the adoption of new management techniques.

In the corporate world, the adoption of new sales methods, the development of new products, reforms in personnel and compensation policy, new production methods, and new funding methods are all examples of structural innovation. The drafting of new policy and its execution, and the addition to and improvement of administrative services, are all examples of structural innovation in governmental offices. Structural innovation in hospitals could range from the introduction of new medical treatment systems to basic conceptual reforms, such as the use of supermarket-style layouts in hospital design.

The Background of Structural Innovation

Two factors demand that a manager undertake structural innovations. The first is change outside the organization. The actions and needs of the recipients of an organization's services are always changing, whether these recipients are the customers of a company, the citizens served by a government office, or the patients of a hospital. The organization must change to meet these changing needs. If a corporation fails to respond to change, it will go out of business; if a public organization fails, it will lose the trust of society.

The second factor is change inside the organization. The constant cycle of hiring, growth, and retirement leads to changes in the distribution of abilities within the organization; the attitudes, values, and behavior patterns of the workers are in constant flux. These changes can cause organizational decay or open a gap between the organization and society. In such cases, the manager must correct the problems with renewed guidance and reform the internal systems of the organization.

The manager must be more than a passive witness to the changes that occur within and outside his organization: he must respond to them creatively and aggressively. This is the true meaning of structural innovation.

Absorbing Cost Increases

Steady increases in the maintenance costs of organizations have placed a premium on the ability of today's manager to effect structural innovation.

Energy and labor costs rise yearly, and the prices of raw materials are skyrocketing. Even organizations that retain the same personnel makeup experience enormous cost increases each year, and there is no end in sight to this trend. The greatest responsibility of all organizations in today's society is to try to absorb these costs instead of simply passing them on to the recipients of their services, be they customers, citizens, or patients. The only way this can be achieved is through structural innovations designed to lower costs while maintaining quality.

In the manufacturing industries, where extreme competitive pressure keeps prices low, various continuous cost-reduction systems have been established, but this sort of indirect management effort has not actually raised productivity enough to absorb rising costs effectively. Most of the service industries lack skill in structural innovation and can only maintain profitability by passing cost increases on to the customer.

Governmental offices are still completely fixated on work quality and have no notion of what it means to take the initiative to lower costs. In the sense that they lower everyone's disposable income, taxes are the biggest single "cost" problem, and the argument that they must always rise, backed up by figures and percentages shrouded in administrative sorcery, is utterly absurd.

Managers of all organizations must first find out the total labor costs and the general management costs of their own sections or departments, and then figure absolutely yearly cost rises based on the yearly settlement of accounts. With the use of structural innovations they must work both to lower these costs and to improve the results gained from any expenditures made.

New and different concepts and methods will clearly be required to meet this goal, which represents the bare minimum of what a manager must achieve through structural innovation. In fact much more is demanded of him.

Types of Structural Innovation

There are three types of structural innovation, defined in terms of how the manager who originates the innovation influences the other parties involved: internal reform, related reform, and strategy advancement.

Internal reform is limited to the internal structure of one section or department; it exists in all sections and departments. In the case of strategy advancement, the staff carries out innovations with the entire organization as the object. Between these two extremes, related reform requires the cooperation of two or more sections or departments.

The manager must first master maintenance management, then set about to effect structural innovations. The nature of structural innovation means that it is different for every section of an organization; the abilities it requires are different from those required by maintenance management. When maintenance management systems are insufficiently developed, reform itself becomes impossible: the whole point of innovation is lost.

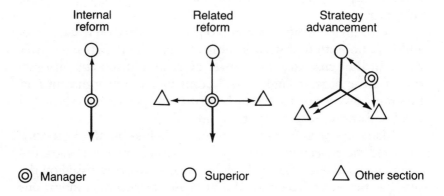

Figure 7. Types of Structural Innovation

Prerequisites of Structural Innovation

Structural innovation has the following prerequisites: negation of present conditions, creating a new unity, getting results, and a sustained effort.

(1) *Negation of present conditions*

Structural innovation means the destruction of existing rules within an organization and the construction of a new order both within and outside the section. The old system is made up of the organizational structure, the workers, the methods they use to perform work, and the underlying operational concepts of the organization. These factors intertwine with one another to form a stable unity, but structural innovation begins with the negation of each of these elements and the search for a new unity.

Organizations tend to move with inertia, and people tend to become psychologically stable in one environment, choosing to avoid changes and unknowns. Both organizations and individuals tend to resist new ideas and new methods.

The manager must bring about structural innovations despite this resistance. He must actively negate present conditions, step out of the familiar old ways, and pioneer new territory. This requires a great deal of determination and power, and the ability to change the thinking of others.

(2) *Creating a new unity*

The second prerequisite to structural innovation is that new concepts and new methods be created.

Whatever new concepts and methods are devised, they must be based on and ideally suited to both the character of the recipients of the organization's services and the internal state of the organization. They must be different from the existing concepts and methods, and they must be creative. They cannot merely be imitations of the actions of other organizations, but must be designed specifically to solve the problems that exist in the originating organization.

> *Japanese industries have a strong tendency to imitate one another: the development of new products, new management policy, the introduction of new management techniques—all of these spread quickly from company to company until they become universal. This tendency has contributed to the raising of*

the country's industrial standards; the same phenomenon may be seen in policy making in local governing and administrative bodies.

Structural innovation, however, involves a thorough examination of conditions within one's own organization and the pioneering of methods specific to its needs. This cannot be achieved through mere mimicry. The only effect of new product demonstrations is to standardize product quality levels and invite excessive price competition. By the same token, it is only logical that the local administrative bodies in different areas should be attacking different problems.

Of course managers should keep an eye on new developments in other organizations and use them as hints for their own activities, but the blind following of trends runs counter to the true meaning of structural innovation. Managers must always aim for reforms that are imaginative, creative, and suited to their specific needs—this is the only way to guarantee the progress of society as a whole.

The best kind of structural innovation is original and completely unique; innovation inspired by something in another organization is second best. Both are certainly valid forms of structural innovation, and it goes without saying that either is a great improvement over being stuck at the stage of maintenance management.

(3) Getting results

Structural innovation is more than just negating the present state of affairs and creating a new one: the result of the innovation must revolutionize work quality and greatly increase the productivity of the section or department. Whatever the form of the innovation, its actual results are all-important.

The various types of administrative reforms enacted in the past have usually emphasized the elimination of a few offices; none has reduced the tax burden or prevented further loads on the budget by actually reducing personnel costs. This sort of "reform" points to the immaturity of the tendencies and the true intentions of the managers and directors involved. Imitation structural innovation only increases costs.

If a manager wishes actually to change the state of affairs within his organization, he must, as part of his structural innovation, mobilize and convince his superiors, his colleagues, the related sections or departments, and his staff. A manager who lacks leadership ability cannot achieve structural innovation. Powerful enthusiasm based on an upright sense of duty and the sufficient ability to transform that enthusiasm into action are indispensable if the innovation is to succeed.

The broader and more sweeping the proposed structural innovation, the more vision and independence are demanded of the manager.

> *Shiseido, Japan's leading cosmetic manufacturer, worked for almost sixty years to build the integrated sales network that was the key to its success: from manufacturer to distributor to chain sales outlet to Shiseido's own promotion and sales organ, the* Hana-tsubaki kai *[Camellia-flower Club].*
>
> *It was in 1918, with the organization of general merchandise chains, that Shiseido initiated its grand scale structural innovation. Until then, the company had not depended on large dealers of general merchandise and had not been fully aware of how distribution channels actually worked. In the twenties and thirties, Shiseido replaced distributors with its own sales organization; in 1936, it established the* Hana-tsubaki kai *as a customer network. This new sales network was destroyed in World War II and later reconstructed; in the 1950s it began to produce results.*

SELF-CHECK

In the organization to which I belong:

- ☐ There are a number of long-term plans in progress that have this sort of vision and originality.

- ☐ There is almost no concern for the long term. We are immersed in the present, and in keeping up with the trends set by other organizations.

- ☐ There are some strategies that could be called long-term, but they do not have vision or originality.

(4) A sustained effort
The fourth prerequisite for structural innovation is that the nature of the section or department be changed.

Organizational units acquire their distinguishing characteristics over time; they reappear repeatedly and are not easily influenced by changes within or without the organization. To reap the benefits of structural innovation, therefore, a sustained effort is required to maintain whatever changes have been made. Tenacity is essential, and special caution is demanded when a manager is replaced by his successor.

In any event, structural innovation means a change from the old to the new. Whatever their merits, the old ways tend to be rigid and resistant to change. The manager must consider how much time it will take to shake the old systems apart and rework them. To succeed in this timing, he must be able to judge the degree to which the individuals concerned are aware of the problem and how much actual desire there is for change. He must strike while the iron is hot.

These conditions govern the effects of the manager's efforts to influence others. It is always possible—to a certain degree—to persuade people of the need for a change before the time is truly ripe. Ultimately, however, a sense of timing that takes into account even the limits of one's own power is the decisive factor in the success or failure of a structural innovation.

To sum up, there are four prerequisites for structural innovation: the negation of present conditions, the creation of a new unity, the realization of results, and the maintenance of a sustained effort. If any of these is lacking, the structural innovation will not succeed.

It often happens in corporations that a good idea is introduced, only to end in senseless argument, or that a good project is begun but ends in total chaos. These failures are judged by the comparable successes or failures of other companies, but from the standpoint of structural innovation, there is nothing worse than to plan without acting, or to act without achieving results.

Four Difficulties for the Manager to Overcome

The president of a western Japan manufacturer of durable consumer goods was dissatisfied that the general managers of his administrative, labor, management, and engineering divisions put almost no emphasis on long-term strategies and instead spent all their time with their respective section managers taking care of routine work.

*The president decided that this situation had developed be-
cause each of these general managers had section managers
under him, so he reorganized the head office accordingly. He
took every employee from section manager down and formed an
in-house service division, under the direct supervision of the
executive director. The general managers became the executive
director's personal staff members. Unfortunately, the result of
this change was that the general managers had no idea of what
they should be doing, and the company soon returned to its original system.*

All managers recognize the importance of structural innovation,
but in practice many remain at the stage of maintenance management, and very few have developed the ability to take the initiative
and effect structural innovations on their own. This is a serious problem from the standpoint of corporate management and can be
traced to four basic difficulties that every manager must overcome:
lack of imagination, insufficient knowledge or energy, lack of persuasive power, and poor management of time.

(1) Lack of imagination

The first difficulty that hinders structural innovation is a lack of
imagination and ideas on the part of the manager. He may be overly
concerned with current issues and rules, and unable to break away
from that level with long-term strategies and new ideas.

Most of today's general managers received their training in
front-line managerial positions during the period of Japan's fastest
economic growth, when they had to give their undivided attention to
maintenance management problems. As a result, though they may be
able to go along with revolutionary ideas from above, they find it
difficult to come up with new ideas themselves, and instead busy
themselves with maintenance management tasks, overseeing the
work of their section managers and entertaining clients. Section
managers have the same limited vision. Both section managers and
general managers are excessively concerned with their own companies and insensitive to the structural innovations occurring in
other companies and other fields.

To enrich their imaginations, these managers must pull away
from their maintenance management functions and mingle with
people outside the company. They must study new management
methods and learn to extract the pertinent lessons from case studies.

The personnel manager is in effect the president of the personnel section; the engineering manager, the president of engineering. They must do more than simply request approval from above for their proposals—they must make opportunities to discuss their ideas freely with the operators of the company, thereby broadening their intellectual horizons. They must never fall into the disgraceful state of knowing less about their own fields than their superiors, and they must also maintain the lead where information and countermeasures specific to their own sections are concerned.

The manager must always see things in the long term; he must have a broader and more future-minded field of vision than the operators of his organization. After all, the operators and directors will leave the organization in time. To the manager, long-range thinking is a self-protective measure—if he neglects it now, he will regret it later.

(2) Insufficient knowledge or energy

Some managers who remain in the stage of maintenance management do not know how to execute structural innovation; others find themselves excessively taxed by the demands of a maintenance management stage.

But what makes a manager a manager is his ability to initiate and lead structural innovation, and the manager who has his hands full with maintenance management is only doing half his job. Such managers must acquire knowledge about structural innovation and work to redistribute their energies. Too many managers lack the ability to make judgments and decisions on their own; they are incapable of original thinking and the comprehensive analysis that must back it up if plans and proposals are to be accepted by higher management. These managers must avoid "intuition-and-modification" thinking and polish their skills of judgment and decision making.

By "intuition-and-modification" thinking, I mean the kind of thinking in which the decision maker examines a problem until an intuitive answer presents itself, and then proceeds to whittle away bits and pieces of his plan as he goes through the process of implementing it. The typical end results is a poor plan: the plan loses its consistency, the best parts of it are lost, and the results of its implementation are unsatisfactory.

(3) Lack of persuasive power

Even if a manager can generally persuade and convince his staff, he may lack the ability to persuade his superiors, colleagues, and those outside the company—particularly when he is trying to present them with an unusual idea and convince them of its validity.

Many managers are aware of their inabilities in this area, and instead of striking out on their own and risking embarrassment, they keep their ideas and suggestions to themselves. Because managers are judged by the degree of their influence within their organizations, however, it is essential that they make deliberate efforts to strengthen their powers of persuasion.

(4) Poor management of time

Some managers tend to become immersed in maintenance management and are content to busy themselves with routine work. Instead of managing their time, they are managed by it. These managers cannot create structural innovations. The mere fact that they are busy is no proof that they are doing their jobs—it shows only that they are poor at managing their time.

At least 70 percent of a general manager's time and 40 percent of a manager's time should be spent preparing for structural innovation: it should be devoted to surveys and the review of hypotheses, discussion and reorganization, and actual leadership of implementation. To reduce the drain on his time, the manager must perfect

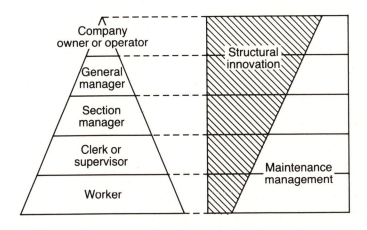

Figure 8. Varying Roles in Structural Innovation by Management Level

maintenance management systems, standardizing work methods and stepping in only to solve unusual problems. He must be able to entrust more work to his staff.

Managers who are already at the stage at which they can autonomously effect structural innovations must strive to become capable of higher-level, longer-range planning. Their full potential is as yet unrealized—they must test the limits of their abilities.

Managers who have reached the stage at which they can participate passively in structural innovations initiated by others need to make a thorough study of how they can get the jump on their superiors. It is pitiful for a manager to know less about his own field or specialty than his superior does. Managers who fall into this category need to change their attitudes and conduct.

Anyone who is still in the stage of maintenance management cannot yet be called a manager. Such individuals must force themselves to spend more time thinking about structural innovation, even if that will require them to delegate more work to those under them.

Needless to say, those who have still not mastered maintenance management must make this mastery their first priority. They must concentrate their full efforts on graduating from the stage of imperfect maintenance management as soon as they possibly can.

SELF-CHECK

Circle the items you think best describe your structural innovation aptitude.

Imagination	good	passing	insufficient
Knowledge	good	passing	insufficient
Persuasiveness	good	passing	insufficient
Time management	good	passing	insufficient

Effecting Structural Innovation

Because the actual content of structural innovation varies with the nature of the department or section, it would be impossible to define a universally applicable how-to method. In general, however, the process of structural innovation must include the following steps:

1. *Investigation:* The manager must investigate both inside and outside the section or department and identify a theme for the structural innovation that must be made.

2. *Decision making:* He must further research this theme, then make decisions on the concepts, methods, people, and systems to be used in the innovation.

3. *Persuasion:* He must convince all concerned of the validity of his concept, prepare people for the changes, get their agreement, and create an atmosphere favorable to the structural innovation.

4. *Implementation:* He must make the final decisions about the details of implementation, continue educating and preparing, and finally make the actual changes.

5. *Evaluation and follow-up:* He must evaluate the results of his implemented structural innovation and follow it up with any necessary modifications and maintenance.

Any structural innovation must include these five steps. This is true for internal reform, related reform, and strategy advancement.

In actual structural innovations, these steps tend to overlap. In the investigation stage, the manager forms hypotheses that are used in the decision-making stage; major persuasion efforts are already under way by the decision-making stage. It is at this point that preparation and implementation are brought out into the open. The time required for the structural innovation varies according to the nature of its theme and the difficulties encountered in the persuasion stage.

INVESTIGATION

The investigation stage of structural innovation begins the day the new manager assumes his position. A change in job brings about a change in mind and is always an excellent opportunity for structural innovation. The newly appointed manager stays aware of changes within and outside his organization as he becomes familiar with his new position and gradually maps out the theme of his structural innovation.

Every manager should adopt two perspectives in selecting and developing the theme for his structural innovation: (1) What does

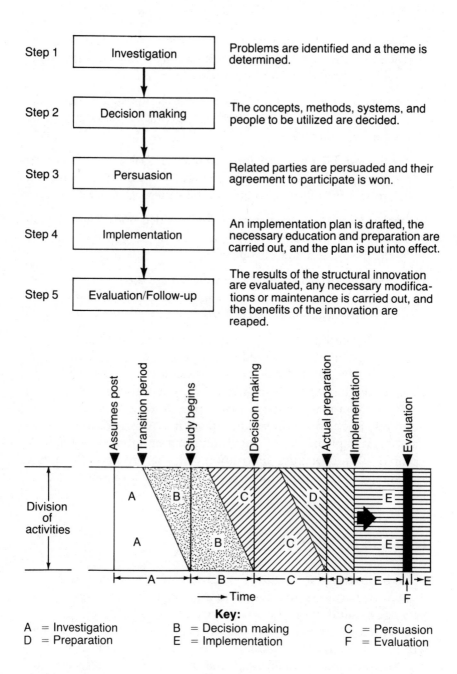

Figure 9. The Process and Stages of Structural Innovation

my organization expect of me in my new position?, and (2) What are the problems in my section or department that I must solve?

To grasp the expectations of the organization accurately, the manager must be extremely sensitive to changes in conditions both inside and outside the organization. When management-related news or information comes his way, he must study it earnestly and try to learn how it relates to the organization's expectations of him. He must never play the idle spectator, assuming it isn't his problem. He must review the periodicals and published information pertinent to his position and formulate views and opinions concerning his organization. Only then can he begin to understand what it expects of him.

To this end, it is important for the manager to hear out the opinions of his staff, colleagues, and superiors, and to be well aware of who is thinking what. This awareness is an important tool in the implementation stages of structural innovation, when the manager must enlist the cooperation of everyone affected.

What's the Problem?

The manager's second perspective in developing the theme of the structural innovation is the problem of his department or section: whatever operational conditions or phenomena the manager must rectify. This problem can usually be defined clearly and concisely.

The Japanese word for problem has several meanings: *problem* can refer to a condition that must be corrected or solved, but it can also refer to the background factors that brought about the condition in the first place. This confusion can present obstacles in actual problem solving. Care must therefore be taken to distinguish problems from their causes.

The problem must be something grounded in fact: the manager's consciousness of problems must not be based on his own subjective tendencies or on the opinions of others. The manager must observe the problem directly at its source and back it up with figures, keeping facts and opinions carefully separated.

The definition of the problem must be concise and comprehensive. The manager should be able to approach his superior and explain in a single sentence the problem he needs to solve. He must not confuse the problem with its causes, and he must never express it in subjective terms. Structural innovation requires the understanding and cooperation of many people in many different positions, so every effort should be made to avoid confusion of this sort in the early stages of problem definition.

One could define the problem as a sort of friction caused by concurrent change in internal conditions and the external environment. Problems of all kinds originate and are then solved in every section of an organization. Those that remain unsolved accumulate and ultimately pose a danger to the organization.

> *Two examples of friction with the outside: in a corporation, sales drop when an excellent product is introduced by a competitor; in a local governing body, internal systems are ill-equipped to deal with a new demand from the citizenry.*

Another type of problem occurs when a gap opens between actual conditions and some ideal held by a manager. Managers with very high ideals see this sort of problem frequently, while managers who tend to accept whatever conditions prevail may not even realize that problems exist. In this sense, managers should not simply discover problems, but should create them by having high expectations.

> *Imagine an accounting department that puts out monthly reports. The accounting manager feels that unless reports are produced by the tenth day of the following month they will not be useful to the operators of the company, but in fact they are currently being turned out on the twentieth day. Another person might simply decide that it is impossible to produce the reports any faster—"that's just how it is"—but to this manager the speed of the reports becomes a problem. It is this sort of problem-consciousness that indicates how much aptitude a manager has for effecting structural innovations.*

Types of Problems

There are four basic types of problems which face every manager.

Problems may first be classified into two groups: *work problems* and *human problems*. Work problems include overstaffing, excessive expenses, sluggish sales, defective products, and uneven work quality. Human problems include poor teamwork, negativity, quarreling, insufficient education, and wrong thinking. In corporations,

Figure 10. Types of Problems

	Current problem	Future problem
Human problem		
Work problem		

work problems may also be called performance problems.

While work problems can usually be represented statistically, human problems tend to defy all but qualitative descriptions. Managers who overemphasize figures and the quantitative analysis of problems therefore run the risk of overlooking human problems.

The other principle of problem classification is between *current problems* and *future problems*. A current problem is one that demands immediate attention; a future problem is one that has not yet surfaced but which is likely, judging from trends and indications, to show itself in a year or more. Some typical future problems include shortages of manpower that could eventually limit a company's ability to fill orders, the danger that a labor-intensive operation will become unprofitable as wages rise, the possibility that conveyor systems will become unduly complex as additions are built onto a factory, and the likelihood that operations will be severely disrupted when a seasoned crew of workers retires and inexperienced workers take over. The manager must distribute his efforts carefully to strike a balance between current problems and future problems.

SELF-CHECK

In my department or section:

☐ I am run ragged by current problems and quite honestly don't have the leeway even to think about future problems.

☐ There are very few current problems, but I need to think about how to attack middle- and long-term problems.

☐ There are both current problems and future problems, and both require attention.

Standards for Evaluating Problems

As long as a manager has high expectations, he will constantly perceive problems. But a manager's time is limited and the duration of his position is short. He must therefore concentrate on the one problem that will allow him to fulfill the concept of "one position, one accomplishment." The key to structural innovation lies in focusing on the most important point.

If many structural innovations are attempted at the same time instead of in a logical sequence, one may cancel out another's positive effects and throw the section or department into confusion. The manager should therefore complete one theme before moving to the next.

As a manager gains experience with structural innovation, however, he may become capable of developing several themes at once. He will succeed if he begins by evaluating his own abilities correctly and concentrates in the early stages of his career on making one lasting contribution in every position he holds.

The manager must sharpen his senses from the day he assumes his new post, recording and absorbing any information or events that might later serve as raw material for his structural innovation theme. He must form hypotheses about problems, causes, and possible countermeasures, and he must follow up these hypotheses, correcting and unifying them and examining the cause-and-effect relationships behind them. When he has taken in a certain amount of information, he should organize it in graph form, drawing up the relationships between problems and their causes to attain an overview of the entire situation. Some managers may find the "KJ method" useful in this process.

The KJ method was developed by Jiro Kawakita. Facts and opinions are gathered and recorded separately on cards, then grouped by cause-and-effect relationship. It is very helpful in solving problems, organizing one's thoughts, and facilitating the participation of others in these processes.

Once the problems are identified and grouped, they should be evaluated according to five criteria: overall contribution to the organization, the manager's own ability, timing, current versus future problems, and work versus human problems.

(1) *Overall contribution to the organization*

In this type of evaluation, the manager asks how great a contribution will be made to the organization if the problem is solved—what the overall effect of its solution will be. Is the solution of the problem appropriate to both the overall policy of the organization and the expectations placed on the manager? This type of evaluation should be made first, and appropriate priority assigned to each problem.

(2) *Manager's ability*

Too often a manager selects as the theme of his structural innovation a problem that ranks very high in priority, but whose solution is beyond the combined abilities of himself and his staff. A good method is to select a problem of secondary priority that can be rapidly conquered: this will build confidence and strengthen the unity of the section. The manager should not exceed his capacity.

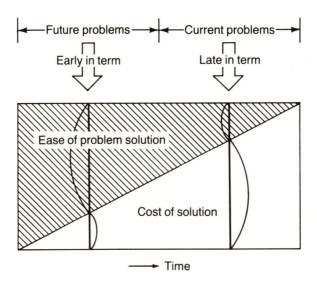

Figure 11. Costs of Problem Solving

(3) Timing

The manager should give priority to problems that seem ripe for solving and those whose solutions are anticipated outside the organization. He should put off until later any problems that if solved too soon might cause internal or external friction. The problems presently being attached in other sections or departments should be considered as well, and integrative or cooperative efforts should be made.

Waiting for the right moment is an important element in problem solving.

(4) Current problems versus future problems

When current problems are serious, they should be given priority. The manager should not become obsessed with future problems when the existence of current problems clearly exist. The manager is not a scholar.

Problems are generally easiest to solve in their early stages; as time passes their solutions become more and more elusive and expensive. Frequently a problem that is barely recognizable when a manager begins a new assignment becomes evident as a current problem by the end of his tenure. Problems that will have significant repercussions when they surface in the future must be given priority as themes for structural innovations.

Very often, steps to counter future problems may be taken during the process of solving current problems. In such cases, higher management may be alerted and involved in the problem-solving process. But future problems demand very clear and deliberate planning. Inexperienced managers often err in judging how fast problems will come to a head.

In the ideal workplace, all major current problems have been solved and everyone is absorbed in solving future problems. The manager must bring about this condition by solving current problems as rapidly as they present themselves and by constantly looking toward the future.

Corporations and government offices tend to differ both in the speed with which they recognize problems and in the timing of their solutions.

Government offices tend to recognize problems relatively

quickly and judge them quite well, but they are usually slow to effect solutions. This is because a government cannot work the solution of a new problem into its budget until that problem has become evident and society at large is aware of it, and also because the government, as the sole provider of social services, need not worry about losing its customers to faster-moving competitors.

However, this is no excuse for foot dragging. In fact, in many cases the high cost of problem solving in governments is in itself the most serious problem.

(5) Work problems versus human problems

Whether a problem is current or future, it is important to assign priorities according to whether it is a work problem or a human problem. These two categories usually influence one another, each alternately causing and being caused by the other. The performance problem of slipping sales can cause the human problem of low morale among sales personnel. Conversely, a dramatic jump in sales can fill the sales department with new confidence and enthusiasm.

It is therefore important, for example, in rejuvenating an operation, to judge which approach will be more effective: a human-oriented one or a work-oriented one. Managers must be sensitive to the cause-and-effect relationship between the two.

The manager must make a comprehensive analysis of the problems at hand and assign them priorities according to the overall contribution to the organization, his own abilities, and considerations of timing. Based on this ranking, and on a carefully balanced approach to the current, future, work, and human aspects of the problems, he must develop the theme for his structural innovation. In the beginning, he should develop one theme at a time; an experienced manager can attack several at once. Throughout the entire investigation stage, the manager must communicate fully with his superiors, his colleagues in related departments, and his staff. All these people must arrive at the final decision on the theme at the same time, and the managers of other sections must understand the theme and be willing to cooperate in its realization.

The investigation stage begins the moment the new manager assumes his position, and again the moment there is any significant change in internal or external conditions. It ends when the manager wins the consent of his superiors and finishes psychologically preparing those under him for the change. The selection of the theme for structural innovation is one of the most important parts of the process: a mistake in this stage can render the later stages meaningless. It is in this selection that the manager's mental abilities are put to the test.

DECISION MAKING

Once the investigation stage is complete and the theme of the structural innovation has been determined, the manager must make final decisions on the concepts and methods to be employed in the structural innovation.

Decision making is the process through which one decides on the actions that should be taken by oneself and one's staff in response to certain prevailing conditions. As part of his maintenance management activities, the manager must confront and solve many individual problems. He makes plans periodically and later decides on which course of action to proceed; he considers proposals and makes decisions on countermeasures to change existing conditions; he deals with any trouble or major problems that arise. All of these are examples of decision making.

The nature of decision making varies according to the decision maker's level within the organization, but in this discussion I will deal exclusively with decision making at the level of manager, as it relates to the structural innovation process. In fact, this is probably the single most important aspect of decision making.

Intuition-and-Modification Planning

One of the most common types of decision-making thinking among Japan's managers is the "intuition-and-modification" type mentioned earlier. The manager approaches a problem and intuitively arrives at a solution. But as he begins to consider the practicality of his solution, he sees that parts of it do not work. He attempts to patch up the plan, or, when there are so many problem areas that it cannot be salvaged, he abandons it altogether.

This is a very common approach, but it is flawed. At its very best, it is unsuited to the all-important structural innovations which every organization needs. Moreover, it invites fundamental errors in the decision-making process. Because the original plan is arrived at through intuition, the planner tends to overlook any other possibilities that may be present. The inexperienced manager has shallow intuitions, and when he is presented with an alternative plan from above, he becomes discouraged. The manager who lacks a sense of the balanced nature of planning and sticks stubbornly to his own intuitive plan is a liability to his organization. Intuition-and-modification planning also often leads the manager to overlook the causative factors behind the problem. As a result, steps taken to alleviate the problem are ineffective. Most problems cannot be solved until their causes have been removed.

SELF-CHECK

My type of judgment is:

☐ Close to the intuition-and-modification method.

☐ Much more objective than the intuition-and-modification method.

☐ Basically intuitive, though I am more prudent when it comes to serious problems.

The Typical Order of Decision Making

Because the manager confronts thousands of different situations, it is difficult for him to adhere to a single pattern of decision making. He must essentially choose the process best suited to the problem at hand. The method described below, however, is fairly universal and relatively foolproof.

1. *Define the problem:* Using the approach described earlier, define clearly the problem you must solve.

2. *Analyze its causes:* Analyze whatever causes or background factors the problem may have. If the problem can be expressed quantitatively, analyze any figures that are available as well.

Problems usually have many causes, and they are usually inter-woven into complex cause-and-effect relationships. The manager must organize his approach to understand these relationships, throwing light on the connection between the problem and its major causes.

3. *Examine the alternatives:* An alternative is a possible solution, a course of action that could be taken, given prevailing conditions. Carefully examine as many as possible. Unlikely alternatives should be discarded and others consolidated and integrated, as necessary, until two or three (or at most four) alternatives remain.

4. *Evaluate and choose:* Compare and contrast the final alternatives and select the one that is most appropriate.

5. *Plan the implementation:* Order all the items and steps necessary for the execution of the alternative plan selected and draft an im-plementation schedule. Then look over the entire plan again, and use your imagination to determine if the steps you have proposed will actually give the results you have predicted. Repair any leaks in the plan, thus completing the final stage of the decision-making process.

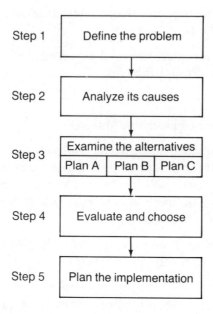

Figure 12. The Order of Decision Making

This process need not be used in dealing with everyday suggestions and proposals, or for plans that can be easily adjusted later on. It should, however, be employed as much as possible for any serious problems: think everything out carefully, write it all down, and discuss it with others.

Start with the Problem

> *Mr. N., an accounting manager, received a visit from the manager of a computer company. The manager wanted to sell Mr. N. an office computer system. He told Mr. N. that if he computerized, he could speed up the schedule of his monthly reports and greatly reduce the workload of the accounting section.*
>
> *Mr. N. took favorably to the idea. He was introduced to the accounting manager of a company that was using the same system, and he sent a supervisor there to investigate. The supervisor came back and reported that the accounting section operated very well, praising the computer system. Mr. N. spoke to the general manager immediately, stating that he wished to form a project team of accounting section personnel and staff members from other related departments to design a new office system that used the computer.*

This manager's approach to structural innovation is totally wrong. The idea of computerizing the accounting section is actually no more than one alternative in the decision-making process mentioned earlier. The accounting section in the other company did not operate well simply because it used computers: computerization itself becomes a viable alternative only when there is some specific problem that it solves. If computers are introduced when there is no special problem that requires them, they will only become a cost liability to the organization.

When Mr. N. heard about the new computer system, he should have taken a careful survey of his accounting operation and the related sections, using any serious problems he found as a point of departure for his thinking. Suppose that he had done this, and that he had found two problems requiring immediate solution: first, monthly reports were late and were not completed until the end of the following month; and second, the present system put a strain on the entire organization at the beginning of every month, and it required excessive manpower.

Next he should have investigated the causes of these problems and come up with several alternative plans for their solution. Computerization would have been one of these alternatives. For example:

Plan A: Speed up the monthly reports by reforming office procedures without the use of machines; reduce personnel.

Plan B: Speed up the monthly reports by ordering changes in the outside data service currently being used.

Plan C: Speed up the monthly reports without changing the present accounting system, but by making other sections submit their bills and other materials earlier than they do presently.

Plan D: Buy a dedicated computer system for the accounting section.

Then Mr. N. should have weighed the advantages and disadvantages of each alternative, selecting the method that yielded the greatest benefits for the lowest cost. This alternative might or might not have turned out to be computerization.

Automation and the introduction of new management techniques have always been a weighty alternative in structural innovation. Unfortunately, many managers start from this alternative instead of starting from the problem itself, and their efforts end in failure. Structural innovation has to start from the problem.

After the manager has defined the problem, he must investigate its background and isolate its causes. He must not rush blindly into any one course of action until he has determined the cause-and-effect relationships behind the problem.

People who do rush blindly into things often think the problems are so clear that they do not require further investigation. This is one of the pitfalls encountered in structural innovation, because both the causes of problems and the ideas of other people involved in them change over the course of time. A careful analysis of the problems and their causes must never be omitted from the process of structural innovation.

The manager must always operate in the correct order: find out what the problem is, find out what caused it, and then find out what alternatives exist for its solution.

SELF-CHECK

☐ My thinking tends to take off from the alternatives.

☐ My thinking always starts from the problem itself.

☐ My thinking depends on the problem.

Examining Multiple Alternatives

There are always several alternatives to consider; there is never just one.

Whatever alternative the manager considers best, there is always some other option. Particularly in corporations, where originality is demanded to surpass competitors, the casual selection of alternatives leads to failure. Many alternatives—the most original ones in particular—must be examined before the selection is made.

A true alternative is based on a unique concept. If that alternative is chosen, all others must be abandoned. All too often, however, the inexperienced manager can visualize only one alternative, or perhaps one alternative and a poor second. Such managers must train themselves to devise new methods, examine all kinds of situations, and spot a number of different alternatives to the problems that exist.

Consider the example of a factory that produces items by individual order: when the demand for a certain product jumps sharply, production capacity is strained. Two possible solutions to the problem come to mind.

Plan A: Expand facilities to absorb the demand.

Plan B: Accept only orders that will be profitable, and fill them using the present facilities.

The two alternatives differ from each other in their conceptual bases—if Plan A were adopted, Plan B could not be. These are the true alternatives in this situation; both of them include a number of secondary alternatives, but these must not be considered on the same level as the alternatives themselves. If these secondary alternatives are approached before the implementation stages, they will merely cloud the issue. The office automation example presented earlier included a number of secondary alternatives.

The examination of multiple alternatives means the examination of the different ways the problem can be approached, and the measures that can be taken relating to each one.

To increase your ability to examine multiple alternatives, you must first master the theoretical concept behind the process. Two methods for this are described below.

(1) Intuitive plan/counterplan/compromise plan

Consider the problem, in a corporation, of how to go about selling a new product. The intuitive plan, call it Plan A, is to use sales agents—this is the method generally used throughout the industry. The next step is to devise Plan B, a counterplan based on a theory totally different from that of Plan A—for example, direct sales. Finally, the planners look for Plan C, a compromise plan somewhere between Plans A and B.

One possibility for a compromise plan would be to break sales down geographically, using agents for certain areas and direct sales for others. The result is that three plans may be compared:

Plan A: Agent sales (intuitive plan)

Plan B: Direct sales (counterplan)

Plan C: Geographic differentiation of sales method (compromise plan)

Many compromise plans are always possible. We are not simply playing with theory here: the intuitive plan is often too common to be effective, and the radical counterplan can sometimes bring unprecedented success. Doing the reverse of what the competitors do can sometimes work wonders, but the implementation of the counterplan requires much courage, and the counterplan itself is often unrealistic because of its extreme nature. This is the significance of the compromise plan.

(2) The third-party approach

Consider your own intuitive plan to be Plan A. Next, imagine what plan your superiors might devise, or what plan might be drawn up by the manager of an impartial section. What might the president of the company do? These plans are predicted, then labeled Plan B, Plan C, and Plan D respectively. The plans are compared, and those based on similar theories are consolidated into one.

This method works particularly well in the reforming of in-house systems, and not so well in other types of structural innovation. If the planner cannot imagine more than one plan, he should actually meet with others and ask them their opinions. If there are individuals who would not offer their opinions even if asked, gather information indirectly and make deductions. The opinions of impartial third parties are important. Any counterplans that come up should be worked into alternatives.

SELF-CHECK

My ability to examine multiple alternatives is:

☐ Below passing.

☐ Quite sufficient.

☐ More or less sufficient, but I have less confidence when it comes to more complicated problems.

Extracting the Lesson Within

Each of the alternatives the manager examines must include some original or unique aspects. If some do not, the manager must make a conscious effort to search for others that do.

To achieve this, the manager must fine-tune his senses until he can extract the salient lessons from his experience—from what he sees and hears, from examples in industries other than his own, and from

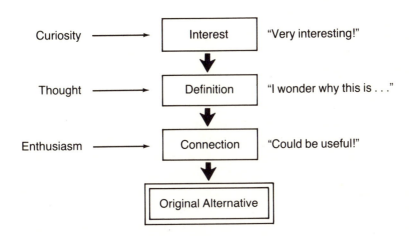

Figure 13. Extracting the Lesson Within

any documents or data he reads—and then link these lessons immediately with his own ideas on structural innovation. Many of
today's most successful executives have a high degree of this ability.

> *Seijiro Ishibashi, the founder of Bridgestone Tire, succeeded
> his father in the family tailoring business early in the twentieth
> century, after which he set up a sock manufacturing business in
> Kurume. On a business trip to Tokyo, the young Ishibashi rode
> the newly constructed trolley and was fascinated by the uniform
> fare system—five sen [5/100 yen] to any point.*
>
> *At the time, socks varied in price according to size, but Mr.
> Ishibashi, taking a hint from the trolley fare, created a struc-
> tural innovation in his trade, and began selling socks at a uni-
> form price regardless of size. He was quickly swamped with or-
> ders and in a short time the small sock maker joined the ranks of
> big business. This structural innovation became the foundation
> of the Bridgestone Tire empire, which progressed from socks to
> rubber-soled work boots, rubberized footwear, and ultimately
> tires.*

The process of taking a hint from outside has historically led to
progress in every imaginable field. To benefit from this process, one
must have fresh, youthful curiosity, the power of thought to unearth
reasons and meanings that may not be apparent, and an enthusiastic
approach to work that will inspire one to draw parallels and make
connections between new things one observes and one's job.

Unfortunately, because of the intensity of the environment in
which they work, managers tend to lose their sensitivity, and their
curiosity may wane with age. They may act as if they understand a
problem when their knowledge is only superficial, they tend to overemphasize action at the expense of serious thought, and they are
hasty to judge things outside their fields as irrelevant.

These pitfalls are the biggest enemy of original thinking and
must be avoided carefully by all managers. Managers must hold on to
their youthful curiosity and get into the habit of thinking deeply
about the meaning of things, then develop the ability to use these resources in conjunction with their enthusiasm for their work to devise
original alternatives. They must make a conscious effort to maintain
contact with people in totally different fields and industries.

SELF-CHECK

How well do you extract the salient lessons from your experience?

☐ I am very inquisitive and in the past have taken hints from other fields.

☐ I would have to say I am not very inquisitive.

☐ Little by little, I have learned to extract lessons from my experience, but I still need to improve.

The ability to extract the lesson within strengthens positive feedback from our experiences by increasing the degree to which we learn from them and by speeding the learning process itself. The ability comes from the right combination of intellectual curiosity, contemplation, and enthusiasm for one's work—a combination that is vital for every manager.

Studying Management Technique

An essential element of the manager's quest for original thinking is a study of management technique and of actual cases from other companies and other fields.

Management technique is a universal "soft" technology, distinct from the "hard" engineering technologies specific to each field. It is a body of thought applicable to all industries, designed to bring about higher work quality and higher productivity in organizations. Management technique has played a major role in the structural innovations in Japan's business world.

What follows is a chronological listing of some management techniques used in Japan, including some that were imported and adapted for use in Japan and some that were developed in Japan. They have their roots in management techniques such as the Taylor system, and branch out into hundreds of different fields and applications.

Time study; motion study; stepped production control; office work analysis; office work improvement; base rate for job class; work sampling; statistical quality control; cost management;

WSP; industrial training; filing; preventive maintenance; controller system; managerial accounting; organization theory; come-up system; marketing (marketing research, product planning, and sales promotion); direct costing; management planning; MDP; factory layout; office layout; business games; case method; EDP; decentralized organization; kanban method; VA; equipment control; unit control; purchasing control; order control; cutting plan; group dynamics; CI; research control; OR; TQC; KJ method; Zero Defects Movement; MIC planning; ST training; skill management; managerial grid; design control; modern IE; PM method; new product development; JK; PAC; material flow control; group technology; self-development; TPM; associate training; managerial strategy theory; structured program; OD; management by objectives; CDP; compiled design; single production line; variety reduction; ABC budgeting; logistics; SPECS; TA; human assessment; scenario method; ZBB; OVA; PPM; SBU organization; contingency plan; project management; matrix organization; MRP; area marketing; AIA; international purchasing; BMP; related management reform; CAD; CAM; international finance; OA.

Each of these soft technologies has its own theoretical and technical structure and its own implementation methods, and all are useful in effecting structural innovations. Regardless of how long ago or how recently the techniques were introduced, each has its own utility. Managers must learn whatever management techniques are relevant to their positions, grasp accurately any new information on management technique that becomes available, attend seminars outside their companies, and be constantly aware of cases and new trends in other organizations.

To apply a management technique, the manager must first gain a clear understanding of the theory behind it. He must then compare this theory with the situation at hand and, without taking it as an immutable truth, develop it to suit his own company. But just as with the introduction of new hard technology such as office computers, he must step back from the alternative and understand the problem itself and its causes. He should only adopt the technique if it is the alternative most likely to solve the problem.

A Comprehensive Judgment

To select the alternative that is the most viable and the best matched to the problem, the manager must systematically compare the strengths and weaknesses of each.

This comparison may be broken down into quantitative and qualitative comparisons. First, the manager should quantify as much as possible the elements of each alternative that can be expressed statistically. For major quantitative design-stage decisions, such as the selection of technology, location, cost-lowering methods, and the reorganization of facilities, basic figures should be examined carefully to determine their soundness. Overly favorable estimates and the deliberate obscuring of figures for the purpose of convincing others of the validity of an alternative are impermissible, for they fulfill personal wishes at the expense of the organization.

The elements of each alternative that can only be expressed qualitatively require comprehensive and conservative study that leaves no room for error. If this basic study is in error, the wrong choice will be made and the manager's reputation will be lost. How error-free a study the manager can conduct is a telling indication of his maturity.

Once the overall priority of quantitative elements such as forecasts, cost estimates, and technical figures is established, the manager must commence studies from an angle compatible with the qualitative elements of his structural innovation. A general rule in assuring success in this stage is to consider what the decisive factors are.

Will the people in charge agree to this? Might there be any obstacles from outside? Could the implementation of the plan cause problems in another section? Though it looks fine for the present, will it have negative repercussions in the future? Will it encourage bad habits? What kind of results will it actually bring? Are there any legal problems with the plan? Each alternative must be examined carefully, keeping in mind whatever risks and difficulties might accompany it.

SELF-CHECK

My ability to make comprehensive judgments is:

☐ Quite sufficient.

☐ Insufficient. I fail to examine problems from certain important angles, and I misjudge their relative importance.

☐ Somewhere between the two extremes.

The process of comparison and selection emphasizes the counterargument. Every alternative has its strengths and weaknesses; in considering an alternative, it is essential to detect any hidden dangers that may lurk within. There is no merit in implementing an alternative to which there is no counterargument; the result is usually the waste of a great deal of time and money. The correct attitude is, "If there is no counterargument there can be no decision." The more original a plan, the more heated an argument it will cause.

Too many managers use the intuition-and-modification method in their decision making. They have difficulty examining many alternatives and making comprehensive judgments, and their thinking tends to lack originality. The level of these abilities in a manager depends on his experience in decision making. He can develop himself by reflecting on his flaws and working carefully on each decision, or by observing carefully how his superiors and those in top management approach decision making. Training by the case method can help here.

Management education through the case method was developed long ago at the Harvard Business School. The student is given case data concerning an actual organization and he acquires skill in decision making through independent research, peer group discussions, and class discussion.

In the decision-making process, a manager must first get the general agreement of his superiors and the understanding of managers in other sections and those outside the organization. He must prepare a plan that documents the problem itself and the strategy, methods, and systems to be used in solving it. In many cases he must make a formal presentation of this plan.

A ceremonial announcement of the final implementation decision is important. By this stage, the bulk of the work of persuading others and enlisting their cooperation must be complete.

It is often useful to employ the services of a management consultant when implementing structural innovations based on management techniques. In such cases, however, emphasis must be placed on both trust and performance. The needs of the organization must be expressed in lucid terms, and the scene must be set within the organization for the changes to come. Progress should be monitored carefully and the final decision should be made at an open meeting.

PERSUASION

The persuasion work of structural innovation is usually conducted in the following order. First the agreement of higher management is won and the cooperation of the section enlisted. Then the organization is primed and prepared for the changes. Finally, those outside the organization are informed of the plan and persuaded of its validity.

Before touching on these stages, however, I will discuss the four fundamental elements of persuasion.

The Four Elements of Persuasion

The manager's persuasive power is one of his most important skills—indeed, it is almost synonymous with competence itself. To use this skill and persuade people effectively, four elements are necessary: *convincing ideas, long-standing trust, a strong will,* and *persuasion technique.*

If a manager hopes to persuade others and have things go as he wishes, he must have relevant, convincing ideas and accurate judgment. He must not fail to consider a viable alternative, nor can he allow blind spots to prevent him from making a comprehensive judgment.

The second requirement for successful persuasion is that there be a relationship of mutual trust between the manager and those he is attempting to persuade. If this trust is not present, even the most commendable ideas will come across wrong. No one in top management will listen to a proposal from a manager he does not trust. Without a solid base of mutual understanding, those in other sections will not cooperate either. In this sense, a manager's persuasive power depends largely on the degree of long-standing mutual trust he shares with others.

The next element of persuasion is the strong will to do what one must by any means possible. If there is a weak spot in your heart you will never achieve this. It should be clear that resolve, enthusiasm, and a strong will are very important elements of persuasion.

The final element of persuasion is technique. The same thing can be said in many different ways, depending on timing, the order in which facts are presented, the approach taken, and the method of expression. Without skillful speech and presentation, persuasion cannot succeed.

Long-Standing Trust

The key in a manager's winning the trust of his superiors is his past performance, how positive his thinking has been and what kind of accomplishments he has made. A manager who has never advanced from the stage of maintenance management will have great difficulty gaining the trust of his superiors.

Another factor that greatly influences the manager's relationship of trust with his superiors is his record of daily communication with them. Even the most capable manager will make his superiors very uneasy if he is careless in his daily reporting and contact with them, or in his consultations with them on plans for the future. In such cases, the lack of information becomes a more serious problem than the proposals themselves.

The care and precision with which a manager performs his work has a strong influence on the trust his superiors place in him. No one wants to make a mistake, but to higher management, small mistakes are cause for big worry, and this worry often leads to mistrust. Top administrators listen to the proposals of managers who are known for the care and precision of their work.

The first and most fundamental element in enlisting the cooperation of other sections is close and long-standing contact. Inaccurate communication and tardiness lead to mistrust and factionalism. A manager's lapses in communication may be interpreted as selfishness or lack of regard for others, and the spirit of cooperation may be lost.

The degree to which the two sections have traditionally cooperated is also important. Unless a manager has always made a sincere effort when called upon by others, he cannot hope to organize the cooperation of others in his own time of need. Organizations stand only through mutual cooperation.

Moreover, contact must have been established before the request. The other section will not be prepared to respond to a sudden call for help. Thus if a manager hopes to enlist the cooperation of another section at some point in the future, he must supply that section with information early on. He can then interrupt this longstanding consulting relationship with a formal request for help.

The same conditions apply to the maintenance of trust with those outside the organization. The manager must deal with these outside parties sincerely, staying in touch and informing them of his plans, supplying them with information that will help them understand his situation, and giving them sufficient lead time before he attempts to effect his structural innovation. The manager must make a particular effort to understand the theories and actions peculiar to each outside organization.

SELF-CHECK

My relationship of mutual trust with other sections:

☐ Is quite sufficient; they will help me anytime.

☐ Is insufficient; I need to start all over again.

☐ Varies with the section.

A Strong Will

A manager must be strong-willed to be persuasive. Those who are known for their persuasiveness are persistent. If they do not succeed the first time, they try a second time, and if that does not work they try a totally different approach. Even with difficult problems, they take time and keep pushing little by little until in the end their intentions have been realized.

It is mere fantasy to expect that problems in structural innovation can be solved at the first attempt. The manager must continue to attack the problem with zeal, taking time and persuading others persistently. Top management is ordinarily the least aware of the activities of their front-line people, so they tend to judge proposals less on actual content and more on the enthusiasm and seriousness of the individuals presenting them.

It is pointless to abandon an idea because of some preconceived notion that "it would never work in this company." Times are constantly changing, as are the internal conditions of all organizations today.

A weak-willed manager will be swept aside in arguments and will be unable to realize his intentions. To succeed, a manager must continue to persuade with firm resolve and unflagging persistence.

Impressive persuasive power alone, however, is not everything. The mark of a seasoned manager is that he builds his case skillfully, side-stepping irrelevant points. Beginners must concentrate first on power of will and then move on to the next level.

> *The founder and operator of a company told me, "The first thing I do when someone brings me a proposal is reject it." According to him, most proposals call for either more money or more people, and they would have put him out of business. If he rejected a proposal once and never heard about it again, he felt he had prevented wasted expense. But when a proposal kept bouncing back no matter how he attacked it, he perceived it as more important. These proposals he considered seriously, paying careful attention to the firmness of the individuals who had brought them up. He reported that the method rarely failed.*

Analyzing the Other Party

The manager must adjust his methods to suit the other parties involved. He must make very careful observations to determine what the other person is thinking and what his worries may be. He must understand the character of the other person to determine whether his approach should be logical or emotional.

Finding out what the other parties' most pressing problems are at the moment is particularly important at the persuasion stage of structural innovation. If there is something about one's own plan that might help the other person as well, the plan becomes much more convincing. To persuade others, it is important to understand not only the individual, but the feelings of his entire group. The failure to understand the feelings of others can lead to the derailment of a structural innovation, no matter how much feeling the manager attempting it may have himself.

Mr. M. was a section manager in the operations staff section of a certain heavy industry, but he was rotated to a position in which he had direct charge of a section performing sales activities. The new division was essentially an in-house sales division, but because of a technological partnership it had been formed as a separate corporation. It was located in the same office with Mr. M.'s original operations section.

When Mr. M. took over the new section, he saw that sales would have to be increased immediately. He decided that the root of the problem was the improper delegation of tasks by the in-section operations manager, and the resulting confusion among the members of the section as to what their responsibilities were. He proposed a vertical division of work by individual that would show the breakdown of results clearly, announced his plan at a full staff meeting, and continued working to convince the various in-section managers. There seemed to be no serious objections, and he officially declared the implementation of the new system. Work was divided among the in-section managers according to their individual specialties, and precise calculations were made of sales, expenses, and profits for each individual.

Unfortunately, the section did not take to the new system very enthusiastically. There were demands for new policies on the merchandise the section handled and many excuses for low sales performance. The negative attitude of the section worsened, and relations soured between those who sold well and those who did not.

Orders ultimately dropped to levels lower than before Mr. M. assumed his post. He tried and tried, but nothing came of his efforts, and two years later he was rotated again. Mr. M. went to another section and the new manager tried a new approach.

Instead of dividing sales according to the individual specialties of the sales staff, the new manager divided the merchandise they handled into product groups, and assigned one sales team to each group. It was at this point that the sales section began to solidify and enter a trend of rapid growth.

The Agreement Process

In winning the agreement of higher management to a structural innovation concept, the validity of the concept itself is obviously a major issue. During this entire process, the manager must take every opportunity to confer with higher management and try to bring them around to his point of view.

At the level of strategy advancement, executives of one section or department work to prime the executives of other sections for a change; they make statements and advance their proposals at meetings and conferences. These executives must therefore see the structural innovation concepts not as favors which their staff managers have asked of them, but as ideas for which they themselves are responsible. They must advance these concepts in the spirit of cooperation with their staff managers.

If a manager's superior is not in total agreement with his plan, the plan will not succeed. Structural innovations meet with many obstacles during the implementation process and risk being shaken apart. During such dangerous times the backup support of higher management is extremely important.

If his superior has only limited influence within the organization, the manager must be particularly cautious if he hopes to effect a structural innovation that will have a major influence on the organization. Since the influence of the superior, and of *his* superior, will be at a premium in the stage of strategy advancement, the manager must consider carefully whose active support will ultimately be necessary for the structural innovation to succeed.

Once his superiors have agreed to a proposal, the manager must work out his strategy and plans. He must consult with higher management on how changes should be made, decide whether the establishment of committees or project teams is necessary from an organizational viewpoint, detect any elements that are crucial to the success or the failure of the structural innovation, and identify the people who will be most instrumental in it.

Priming Others and Setting the Scene for Change

For either related reform or strategy advancement, though not for structural innovations that are limited to his own section or department, the manager must prepare and prime others for the reforms he is about to make, and set the scene for change in the organization. The priming of other sections or departments for change proceeds through two stages: first, the organizing of core members; second, general preparation.

The core members are those few people who will cooperate with the manager effecting the structural innovation and actually participate in its implementation. They are the managers of other sections with whom the structural innovator has kept in constant contact, consulting with them and hearing their opinions; they have been in agreement with the overall concept of the structural innovation since before the persuasion stage. The further-reaching the structural innovation, the more essential a role the core members play.

In the second stage, the core members are used as a lever to win the agreement and understanding of those they influence. This must be done fairly, to avoid any misunderstanding as to the motives of the proposal.

Find a key person. Find someone who can successfully realize the structural innovation, and spend enough time to get his full understanding and his active agreement. If there is a possibility that this key person could instead become a powerful opponent, proceed carefully, step by step, from concept to method.

It is at this point that the manager must obtain information on any procedure or course of action that may prove necessary. In some instances, it may appear that the structural innovation will require either more or less time than originally anticipated.

Both before and after he makes the formal announcement, the manager must set the scene within his organization for the changes he plans. This he must accomplish through any means he can devise. Lectures in the organization by outside specialists and authorities often impress higher management and are therefore very useful in creating a favorable climate for change. Some other useful techniques for initiating internal changes include sending a staff member to study at an outside organization and having him come back to report on what he has learned, or sending study teams to other companies or abroad and leading discussions upon their return. In any case, the only way a manager can bring others to a correct understanding of his plan is to expose them to the same information he used to formulate it. Internal reports and departmental meetings are two more useful tools.

When it is important to persuade and convince individuals outside the organization, they should be handled in the same way as the internal employees. Meetings should be set up for the specific purpose of discussing the structural innovation, and the individuals should be briefed on the changes to be made. The manager who wishes to effect a structural innovation must never forget that no one else understands it as well he does, so he must be prepared to do whatever is necessary to set the stage for the changes it will bring.

SELF-CHECK

How good are you at priming others for a major change?

☐ Pretty good, I think.

☐ This is a problem for me; I need to get better at influencing those outside my section.

☐ It depends on the other person.

IMPLEMENTATION AND EVALUATION

Implementation Planning

The implementation plan is prepared on the basis of careful discussion with section members, committees, and the executive offices.

At this stage, the elements of the plan are enumerated, responsibilities are delegated, and an overall schedule is drafted, listing all the elements of the plan chronologically and according to the individual responsible. The schedule should cover a minimum of six months, or, for large-scale projects, five or ten years or more. The entire process is broken down into stages, objectives for the end of each stage are established as quantitatively as possible, and the time frames for each individual element of the plan are clarified.

At each stage of this process, any obstacles that might arise must be anticipated and steps taken to prevent them from hindering the implementation of the structural innovation. These potential obstacles include anything that might distract the individuals involved during the period.

Another important step is that activities connected with the structural innovation be kept in careful equilibrium with the maintenance management activities of each group involved, both within the section and outside it. Many failures in the implementation stage are due to an excessive emphasis on structural innovation activities, with the ultimate result that unfinished daily chores pile up and impede the innovation. In cases where it seems that workers will not be able to achieve an effective balance, special teams should be organized or the current division of responsibilities should be temporarily altered. If changes are made in the division of responsibilities, each individual must understand them accurately.

Model Runs and Education

In many cases, experiments and model runs should be conducted for specific parts of the plan before the full-scale structural innovation is undertaken, and implementation details should be worked out on the basis of these trials. Examples include the test manufacture of new products and market tests, the setup of pilot plants when new equipment is being developed, and simulations of various new system designs. In the pilot system, frequently used in reforms of factories or sales networks, the new methods are implemented in one part of the organization, results are achieved there, and the reforms are continued throughout the organization using the pilot as a model from which all may learn.

In the implementation stage of structural innovation, the education of all those involved is extremely important. Implementation manuals and instruction booklets describing in detail the concepts and the methods to be used in the structural innovation must be prepared and the entire organization educated through them.

It is essential to give sufficient time and preparation to education. A great deal of energy must be devoted to changing the ideas and concepts of others. No matter how much he educates others, however, no one understands the structural innovation as well as its initiator, so he must redouble his educational efforts—sometimes even to a point that will try the patience of his "students."

The initiator of a structural innovation must allow enough time for the preparation of educational literature, audio-visual materials, and on-site training.

Evaluation and the Future

Structural innovation requires the prior establishment of methods to measure the success of the project over time. At each preestablished measuring time, the progress of the structural innovation is judged and any necessary minor adjustments made. If a committee presides, the results of these measurements are reported and careful observation is continued. The success of large-scale reforms depends less on conditions at the starting point than on the continued efforts of all involved. In many cases, truly revolutionary results are achieved gradually, by continuing efforts into the future and expanding the plan each year.

A great deal of skill is required for the continued expansion and development of a structural innovation plan. This sort of continued effort is often endangered when a new manager takes over the initiating section. Top administrators and higher management must be extremely careful to maintain a powerful leadership effort until the structural innovation has completely solidified and its benefits have been realized.

SUMMARY OF CHAPTER 4

1. Structural innovation means a reform in the operation of one's section through the introduction of new concepts and new methods, for the purpose of improving work quality, raising productivity, and creating a new unity within the section. Structural innovation means the fruition of the concept of "one position, one accomplishment."

2. Structural innovation not only helps the organization respond to internal and external changes, but enables it to strike out on its own and pioneer new paths. Particularly today, when organizations are faced with continuing increases in costs, managers must at the very least effect structural innovations that allow their own sections to absorb these rising costs, and to achieve results that more than balance them out.

3. There are four essential elements of structural innovation: the ne-

gation of present conditions, the creation of a new unity, the realization of results, and the maintenance of a sustained effort.

4. The manager must conquer four basic difficulties to effect a successful structural innovation: lack of imagination, insufficient knowledge or energy, lack of persuasive power, and poor management of time.

5. Five stages must generally be completed to accomplish any structural innovation: investigation, decision making, persuasion, implementation, and evaluation/follow-up.

6. In the stage of theme investigation, the manager must understand fully both his organization's expectations of him and his section's problems. He must break down the problems into current problems and future problems, then identify the most important points of each problem through pertinent evaluation. The objective of every manager is to solve current problems immediately and thereby create an environment in which he can devote his fullest attention to future problems.

7. In the stage of decision making, the manager must abandon the intuition-and-modification method and start with a definition of the problem. He must train himself to analyze the causes of the problem, examine multiple alternatives, and, making a comprehensive judgment, select the most viable alternative from among them.

8. The alternatives must always include some that are original. To this end, the manager must venture outside his organization and deepen his contacts with those in different fields; polish his ability to extract the salient lessons from what he experiences; place sufficient emphasis on the study and application of various management techniques, case studies, and surveys of other organizations; and to the best of his abilities prepare plans that are unique.

9. To persuade others, the manager must have convincing ideas, longstanding relationships of mutual trust, a strong will, and a mastery of the techniques of persuasion. He must make scrupulous efforts to win the agreement of his staff and his superiors, to prime others in the organization for the reforms he plans to make, and to set the scene for change.

10. At the implementation stage, the manager must formulate his implementation plan on the basis of experimental models and pilots. He must foresee any potential obstacles and take steps to prevent their interference, and he must plan appropriately to ensure that structural innovation activities are not impeded by maintenance management activities. The thorough education of all involved is a key element in the success of structural innovation.

11. After implementation, the manager must take periodic measurements and evaluate the success of the structural innovation. Any necessary adjustments or additions must be made, and a firm leadership effort must be maintained until the full benefits of the structural innovation have been reaped. The manager must keep in mind that the transfer of key personnel is especially dangerous to the successful continuation of structural innovation activities.

PART THREE

The Human Aspect of Managing

The three major elements of the human aspect of the manager's job are trust, motivation, and development. These three are deeply interrelated: if there is no trust, there can be no motivation, and efforts to develop workers will only succeed when they are totally involved with their work.

Chapter 5

Trust

Trust is the foundation of the human aspect of the manager's job. The manager must establish relationships of mutual trust with his workers, his colleagues, his superiors, and those outside his organization. The discussion in this section will center on the first of these relationships, the one he shares with his workers.

THE MANAGER'S CHARACTER

Selfish or Selfless?

The single greatest influence on the manager's relationship of mutual trust with his workers is his character, or his personality.

This does not mean that the manager is expected to be a perfect human being. Like anyone else he has his flaws and his attractive qualities. There is one point, however, on which no concessions can be made. A manager cannot be selfish. If he is, his workers will smell him out immediately.

The selfish manager fobs off all the unpleasant or annoying work on his staff, doing only those jobs that make him look good; is dishonest in money matters; takes the credit for his workers' accomplishments; flatters his superiors but harasses his staff; and worries about his own "score," devoting energy only to those tasks he thinks will win him "brownie points."

If a manager has no real feeling for his workers and tends to think of them only as tools to get the work done, he will inevitably earn their mistrust. The manager's true function is a selfless one. He must to a certain extent forget his own desires and work to develop his workers so that they can excel wherever they go in the future.

The selfish manager is destined for failure. This kind of person has no business being in a leadership position in the first place.

Enthusiasm for Work

Another factor that strongly influences a manager's relationship of mutual trust with his workers is his own enthusiasm and love for his work. People are moved to action by the enthusiasm of others. If the workers perceive that their manager works with diligence and enthusiasm, and that he thinks about the future and studies hard, they will eventually come to feel that they too must work hard. Even if this makes them feel somewhat awkward at first, their feelings of commitment will strengthen and grow. If, however, the manager himself seems less than completely committed to his work—for example, if he comes in late to the office, works lackadaisically, or is always preoccupied with things other than his work—this will immediately affect his staff. Despite the appearances they may keep up, they will soon hold him in contempt.

A manager's enthusiasm for his work is an indication of his sense of responsibility and duty, and of his own consciousness of his position. For the manager, whose job is to motivate others, enthusiasm is an indispensable qualification.

A manager who is always constructive and who approaches difficult problems by looking for positive solutions will raise the level of trust his staff has for him. No worker will trust a manager who pretends to listen to staff members but then disregards any suggestions from them that might increase his own workload, or, for that matter, a manager who thinks only about ways to keep collecting his pay with a minimum of effort. No matter how adverse the circumstances, even if he is on the verge of retirement, the manager must act positively and constructively according to what he believes. This is when he shows his true mettle.

Fairness and the Distinction Between
Company and Personal Matters

Another important element in winning the trust of one's workers is the maintenance of a rigid distinction between company and private property and time.

The manager must be fastidious about the separation of company funds and personal funds, and never abuse company funds under any circumstances. He must not use workers for personal business, even if they offer their services. A confusion in the distinction between "company" and "personal" is a fatal error for a manager, who must always keep perfectly clean. It should be clear from Japanese industrial history that the misappropriation of company funds by top management can easily lead to the bankruptcy of even a long-established company. Misappropriation of funds by top executives sets an example for the rest of the organization. The same is true of managers.

The manager must be fair and unbiased toward everyone, and he must treat people properly. The manager who puts labels on people or who seems unreasonably harsh and unforgiving will ultimately be censured for his own lack of maturity.

The manager must be honest. He must always be sincere, never two-faced. When he deserves blame, he must accept it. He must be modest and humble about all things. All of these elements strongly influence the workers' feelings of trust in their manager.

A manager is no more than a human being, and it is therefore unreasonable to demand that he be flawless. But he must have at the very least the three qualities described above: he must be unselfish and work for the sake of others; he must have enthusiasm and feeling for his work; and he must keep company and personal matters strictly separated.

Because the manager's position makes it hard for others to point out even his clearly apparent faults, he must have above all the ability to evaluate himself. Many people flatter him, but few offer him constructive criticism, so if he is not careful he will run the risk of becoming self-satisfied and committing grave errors.

THE MANAGER'S INFLUENCE WITHIN HIS ORGANIZATION

The Ability to Influence Higher Management

Workers are generally quite sensitive to how much influence and persuasive ability their managers have in dealing with the other managers and executives in the organization. Today, a manager who cannot influence his superiors or enlist the cooperation of other sections will be considered incompetent by his own staff.

The manager must not justify his own inability to persuade his superiors by claiming that they are hardheaded. A manager who says he cannot do anything unless the higher-ups approve will earn the contempt of his staff. And since the manager's job in the first place is to influence others, this contempt is well-deserved. Such managers are merely preserving the outmoded tradition of the high-ranking servant. They have not yet understood that the manager must function as the president of his section or department.

Views and Beliefs

If workers get the impression that their manager has no views of his own and is merely being controlled by his superiors, they will lose their trust in him.

When decisions made by a manager are frequently reversed, his workers will slow down and become unable to work. It is only natural that they will lose their desire to work if they feel their efforts will be wasted. The manager must have clear beliefs and a firm character that will not be shaken by outside pressure.

THOROUGH BACKUP

The manager must be well aware of the conditions his workers face; he must know who is having difficulty with what and where.

When he sees that his workers are facing a problem they cannot conquer by themselves, he must give them backup support and help them to succeed. The importance of such support was described in the earlier discussion on building a favorable work environment. Workers will be afraid to work for a manager who seems to encourage them but does not follow through in the end. If the manager fails to cover for even one worker, he will instantly lose the trust of his workers.

The manager must know the workplace inside out. He must be well aware of where problems may arise if there is some change in internal or external conditions. He must be able to judge accurately where his support is required and in which situations he should leave his workers to their own devices. When he is needed, he must be there instantly; his timing must never be poor. His effort in all of these areas determines his workers' trust in him.

Many other factors also influence and control the degree to which a manager's workers trust him. Even after he has gained their trust, a negative event could become a turning point in the relationship and change their feelings to mistrust.

Ultimately, however, it is the manager's character that determines how much he is trusted. The manager is completely transparent to his staff, however he may try to hide from them. There is nothing more he can do than to act as he feels he must, in accordance with his beliefs as a human being.

SELF-CHECK

To achieve mutual trust with my workers, I need to make more effort to (check more than one if applicable):

☐ Reflect on my own character and change the ways I act.

☐ Improve my ability to persuade my colleagues and superiors.

☐ Provide my staff with thorough backup support.

Chapter 6

Motivation

THE MEANING AND NATURE OF MOTIVATION

Influencing the Workers

Motivation means stimulating workers and creating an environment in which they can become totally involved in their work.

The primary element of motivation is a manager's influence on his workers, both as individuals and as a group. This influence has both direct and indirect forms. Direct influence means spurring the workers into action—for example, talking directly with a worker who may be wavering and encouraging him. Indirect influence means setting up some sort of scheme that will encourage the workers to take action independently. The manager can establish a group objective, institute a system that will provide a stimulus in economic form, or remove any factors that obstruct the workers' will to work. The manager can take the helm and make the atmosphere of the workplace more productive.

In any case, the manager must do something to incite his workers to work. He will never achieve this goal by simply sitting there.

The second element of motivation is creating a workplace environment in which the work is so interesting to the workers that they simply cannot get enough of it. If the workers find their jobs interesting they will give the work their all; they will face every task positively and never feel burdened by their work. The work takes on its own rhythm, and this rhythm becomes a source of pleasure.

If a worker does not find his work enjoyable, every minor set-back will deepen his aversion to it and make him more negative. He will try to avoid difficult tasks and not involve himself at all in his work.

The third element of motivation is creating an environment in which the workers independently help one another. Not only are they positive and interested in their work, but each member of the group performs his function correctly, making it easier for the others to perform their functions.

Group teamwork not only brings the joy of accomplishment, but also deepens the trust among the members of the group. The group then takes pride in itself and takes pleasure in facing new prob-lems together.

The manager must therefore devote great care and effort to building such a group—one that is filled with positivity and intimacy on the individual level and bound together as a whole with mutual trust.

Bringing Out the Buried Will to Work

With the exception of a very small minority, almost everyone in Japan's companies has the "will to work." Everyone who takes a job in a new organization tries as hard as he can to win the trust of his peers and to become an indispensable presence in his workplace. This is one of the best features of Japanese society.

But suppose that after a while a worker seems suddenly to have no desire whatsoever to work. This does not necessarily mean that he has lost his will to work, but merely that something is acting to obstruct that will and he is temporarily unable to display it. It is very common for a person who was once negative to regain his energy suddenly after a change in job, peers, or superiors. With the rare ex-ception of pathological conditions, when someone seems to have lost his will to work it is usually no more than a temporary slump.

Removing Individual Obstacles

Many factors can obstruct an individual's ability to display his will to work normally.

Some examples are: when the boss is unfair, and the worker always feels he is at a disadvantage; when a worker cannot trust his boss and therefore feels there is no point in working hard; when a worker's basic training is incomplete, he fails at whatever he does, and he loses confidence and becomes negative; when he is given a job too difficult for him, receives no support from his boss, and loses confidence; or when he has never done anything more than mechanically perform the tasks assigned him, and has therefore never taken any pleasure in his work.

There are individuals whose personal troubles interfere with their work; others are preoccupied with things outside their jobs and become absent-minded. Workers may become depressed or neurotic and resist even coming to work; they may fail at something and become defensive; they may feel victimized. In some cases a worker may dislike a certain co-worker so strongly that he doesn't even want to see the other's face.

Motivation means stripping away these obstacles and allowing each individual's normal will to work to show through.

Every individual is unique, and so each one's obstacles differ from those of others. Even within the same individual, the obstacles change with time. The manager must therefore grasp each worker's obstacles accurately and take whatever action is necessary to remove them.

Because managers spend their days in a tense working environment, they sometimes make hasty judgments about difficult workers. They may sometimes wrongly judge a worker as having no will to work. This, however, is wrong thinking. Instead, the manager should look for some obstacle that is obstructing the worker's normal will to work, and he should try to discover a way to remove the obstacle. This is where a manager's skill is truly put to the test.

SELF-CHECK

Are you the type of manager who judges from appearances and decides that his workers simply don't have the will to work?

☐ I guess I am.

☐ I never judge by appearances; the first thing I do is look for obstacles that might be obstructing their will to work.

☐ I don't make snap judgments, but there are some cases in which I just can't see it any other way.

THE PREREQUISITES FOR MOTIVATION

Correct Your Own Bad Habits

The first prerequisite for motivation is that the manager have the full *trust* of his workers. When there seems to be a motivation problem in the section, this is the first thing to check.

The second prerequisite is *good managerial habits*. Before deciding that a worker has a motivation problem, the manager must ask himself whether he has any bad habits that might be making his workers lose their desire to work for him. Managers are people too, and therefore have all sorts of idiosyncrasies. Among these are various bad habits that can discourage workers, incite them to negative actions, douse their newly-kindled will to work, and make them generally unhappy with their jobs.

Many bad habits can extinguish the enthusiasm of a worker. If a manager insists that work be done perfectly and is excessively strict about small mistakes, his staff may lose its will to work. This can happen even if the manager is not given to fits of anger—just frowning at every problem does enough damage. If a manager tends not to show interest in the original ideas and experiments of his workers, the entire group's will to work may atrophy.

From the workers' point of view, many managers have bad habits. Just think of your own superiors and the point should be clear. If you cannot think of any bad habits they have, it is safe to assume that you just haven't noticed them.

> *Mr. M. had a particularly conspicuous habit. When any of his workers made a mistake, he would call in that person, ask him what had happened, and then harangue him vehemently. "It's all your fault!" he would say. "You'd better shape up and do a more careful job! This isn't the only time you've screwed up—you did the same thing three months ago! And then the same thing once before, at the end of last year...." In this way,*

Mr. M. would berate the worker, dragging up from the past every mistake he had ever made.

Most of the workers who were reprimanded in this way became quite depressed. Though Mr. M. noticed their response, he said nothing. He figured that they would recover, and that if they didn't, they were just weaklings and there was nothing he could do about that.

Mr. M. himself was a hard-working manager and felt it was a waste of time to warn workers each time they made a little mistake. He would therefore store up incidents in his memory and when he thought the time was right, let everything out at once. He didn't see this as a wild outburst of pent-up anger—he didn't consider himself the emotional type. But his staff came to think of him as a terrifying man, and they began to do everything with excessive caution.

I learned of another incident while talking with Mr. M.:

When he was still a section manager in planning, before he had become a general manager, Mr. M. had a problem worker in his section. The worker had graduated from a good university and was very capable, but he had a tendency to be overly independent and could not work as part of a team. His peers did not like being put in the same group with him and they began to isolate him.

Mr. M., as a section manager, had warned the worker many times, but to no avail. He finally decided that the worker was beyond his control and gave up on warning him, but the same problem kept coming up over and over again. Eventually, Mr. M. lost his patience and exploded, "What the hell do you think you're doing? Aren't you old enough to know better than this by now? How many times do I have to tell you? It's the same thing as before all over again! It's just like I told you before!"

The worker was apparently shocked by this dressing-down from the section manager, and his bad habit vanished. Mr. M. took this to mean that people's bad habits are not corrected with a simple warning here and there. His belief was confirmed that unless you really blow up at them it won't do any good.

There is a very important lesson in this story. The fact is that no textbook can teach a manager how to direct people. A manager must teach himself through his own experiences. If a method succeeds, he will consider it successful; if it fails, he will abandon it. In other words, a manager's firmest beliefs are based on his own limited experience. This is how cases like Mr. M.'s arise. By a fluke, his method succeeded, and so he thought it was the best method. Unfortunately, however, his workers saw it as no more than a bad habit, and whenever his temper flared up they would stand back and think, "Oh, no, there he goes again."

It should be very clear from this example that everyone has at least one bad habit he needs to correct.

I see a bad habit that is fairly common to the managers of corporations and all kinds of organizations. An increasing number of managers deal with their workers only on the level of work, offering neither praise or warning. But everyone is concerned with how his superior regards the job he is doing. If there is no reaction from above—positive or negative—the worker will begin to feel anxious. He will begin to feel that his manager has no concern for him as a human being and will eventually lose trust in that manager.

The foundation of managing is the response a manager gives to those under him. The values of the workplace are determined by the praise and the warnings of the manager. Today's workers are very sensitive; they are not so simple as to think that everything must be all right if the work is done and no one says anything about anyone else. To the contrary—such a situation undermines trust and can lead to the destruction of the work environment.

Everyone wants the work to go well. But if a manager tries to avoid any kind of contact or friction with his staff, he will instantly be seen through. Just thinking his staff is doing a great job is not enough—if he does not express this clearly they will never become enthusiastic. It is a very serious bad habit of today's managers to withhold both praise and blame.

SELF-CHECK

☐ I have some bad habits that might rob my workers of their will to work.

☐ I can't think of any bad habits, but my workers might think I have some.

☐ I can safely say I have no such bad habits.

Dealing with Negative Factors Within the Organization

We have discussed trust and the habits of the manager, but there is one more problem in motivating workers: negative factors within the organization that the manager cannot control.

For example, workers may feel conditions are unfair because pay scales are too low or because facilities are poor. There may be dissatisfaction because of an unreasonable promotion, or because of the perverted equality of the seniority method of promotion. The workplace may be stifling because of poor labor-management relations, and worker mistrust of the top administrators of the company may fall on managers as well. There may be cliques whose members are more concerned with one another than with their work, or strong factionalism that causes friction between sections.

Such conditions are extremely unpleasant for the manager who is making a serious effort to do his job, but he cannot ignore their existence. What then should he do?

The first thing the manager must do is *accept the adverse conditions and make an effort to improve them,* without using them as an excuse for his workers' lack of enthusiasm. Even if the entire organization suffers from these conditions, their influence will vary from section to section depending on the efforts of each section's manager. All this means is that the manager must work harder than usual to motivate his workers—it is not a question of "all or nothing." This is another situation where the manager's abilities are put to the test.

The second thing he must do is *enlist the cooperation of the managers of other sections in dealing with the negative factors.* Most of these problems should be solved by top administrators, but if the manager is in a position where he suffers because of them, he must not remain silent.

Conquering negative factors within the organization takes time. The manager must be persistent and rejoice in small improvements. He must join with like-thinking managers and continue the effort to improve things.

MOTIVATING INDIVIDUALS

The manager must take two approaches to motivation: the *individual approach* and the *group approach*. I will discuss the individual approach first.

Recognize Each Individual's Strongest Points

The first thing a manager must do to motivate individuals is to develop the habit of viewing each individual in terms of his strongest points.

Because managers work in a hectic and demanding environment, they are apt to notice a worker's weakest points first when they meet him. The transmission of feelings between people who work together is a very subtle and mysterious thing. When a manager detects his worker's weaknesses, the worker somehow senses this and feels uncomfortable. In some cases, this feeling can throw the worker into a vicious cycle and he will not be able to perform.

It is very important, therefore, to focus first on people's strong points. Everything begins from a positive recognition of a person's best qualities and an affirmation of his potential to develop them still further. The manager who realizes this gives his workers strength and makes it possible for them to approach the unknown with confidence. This is a fundamental requirement for managers; nothing will ever come of lamenting the character or abilities of a worker or of cutting him down with sarcastic remarks.

When a manager spots a weakness in a worker whom he is meeting for the first time, he must ignore the weakness and consciously look for strong points. Everyone has some strengths. When the manager finds these strong points, he must praise them openly.

A worker is naturally nervous when he meets his new manager for the first time, but this technique will relieve his nervousness and make him feel that, since he has been accepted, he will now have to work hard. This is an extremely important element in the manager's individual relationships. If good communication is established from the start, there will no problem later even if it becomes necessary to warn or reprimand the worker.

If a manager thinks something but never says it, it will be as if he had never thought it in the first place. A manager can always initiate good communication by openly praising a worker. The human relationship is all, and the start of that relationship is extremely important.

How to Make Work Interesting

There are many different jobs in the workplace. Some are interesting to everyone, and some, apparently, to no one. But the more important realization is that work itself is made either interesting or unpleasant by the attitude of the person doing it.

Two people can do exactly the same job, one loving it, the other hating it. In this sense, the judgment of work as either interesting or unpleasant is a very subjective thing. There is a way to make work subjectively interesting. People who enjoy their jobs have learned this method through their own experience.

There are three typical methods of making work interesting, which we might call independence, measurement, and the pursuit of targets.

(1) Independence—letting workers play the lead in their work

The first method is to make workers abandon the notion that they are doing work someone has ordered them to do, and consider instead that they are giving themselves the work. Pastimes and sports are always fun, because we are our own boss. Because we do what *we* decide to do, we enjoy yourselves; if we are forced to do something, it is no fun. The same is true of work. If a worker is merely ordered to perform tasks it is no fun, but if he tells himself to do the work, it becomes enjoyable.

In this modern age, in which our egos are highly developed, independence is the fundamental prerequisite for experiencing pleasure. If we feel that we are having an effect on our environment and that we are controlling our work instead of it controlling us, we will feel favorably disposed toward doing it. But if we can make no effect on our environment and are merely following rules or doing what we are told, we will never derive any pleasure from our work.

It is especially important to teach new employees not to be used at work, but to play the lead in their jobs and to work in freedom, mastering their jobs instead of being mastered by them. It is essential that the manager teach them these skills so that they can learn how to enjoy their work early in their careers.

(2) Measurement—keeping score

The second method of making work interesting is to measure one's progress in it. We always keep score in some way in our sports and hobbies. In work too we can plan our next move on the basis of the score we achieved with the last one.

Operations managers have scores: sales and income rates, expense rates, and other economic figures. In a factory, score can be kept by recording the defect rate, delivery time, or the amount of goods manufactured per person. Each employee keeps score on himself; he comes up with new ideas based on his past record, applies these new ideas, and sees how they affect his score. The pleasure of the repetition of this process is the same for both work and play. The way to make work fun is to think of new ways to do things, try them out, and then repeat the cycle by thinking of more new ways.

It is good to get into the habit of scoring one's on-the-job performance, even with jobs that seem hård to score. Management and administrative jobs may seem difficult to measure quantitatively. On the other hand, because such jobs do not have the same type of group objectives as line production jobs, they are much better suited to individual score-keeping.

The fundamental difference between sports and work is that while sports have rules, at work we make our own rules. Managers should help their workers learn to keep their own scores independently. If the workers find this too difficult, the managers must give them advice and help them arrive at their own rules.

(3) The pursuit of targets

The third method of making work interesting is to set targets and then pursue them. In the game of *go,* we give our opponent a certain number of squares, decide on the game rules, and then fight it out. It is fun if we win, and even if we lose, it is interesting to scheme and struggle along the way.

The equivalent of the "handicap" in work is the target we set for ourselves. Ideally we might have an accurate handicap system based on other workers in the same positions in other companies, but since that would be too difficult to arrange, we set targets for ourselves—by a certain time, I will bring about a certain condition—and we fight it out.

The interesting part of a target is the process of trying various new ideas to achieve it, and then either succeeding or failing. Once a target has been achieved, it is no longer interesting to achieve it a second time. To keep work interesting over a prolonged period of time, therefore, one must get into the habit of setting a new target as soon as it becomes clear that the present one will be achieved. One must always keep oneself in the middle of this process.

It is the manager's foremost responsibility to teach young work-

Figure 14. Making Work Interesting

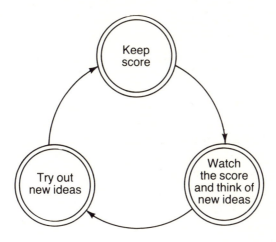

ers that the mastery of methods to make work interesting is an issue of lifelong importance.

Dealing with Problem Workers

Every section has a problem worker who just does not want to do his job.

The manager must approach such workers and correct this problem. He must talk with the worker, find the source of the problem, and rekindle the worker's natural will to work.

The classic method is to meet with the worker somewhere away from the workplace and hear him out completely. Because the problem could be almost anywhere—work, private life, school, family, or interests—the manager must fully understand the worker's overall situation. The manager must not interrupt; he must be a good listener. People who have no will to work tend to be closed and withdrawn. By hearing such people out, a manager can open their minds again and remove the obstacle that is burdening them.

If the worker does not open up at the first meeting, or if the roots of his problem do not come to light, the manager must keep meeting with him and become personally closer to him. Then he can take steps to remove the obstacle. For some workers, talking may have a cathartic effect that acts as a turning point.

If the cause of a worker's indifference is that he does not know the basics of his job (a particularly common problem in sales), the manager should teach him again. If it is that he has no confidence because his work is too difficult, the manager should give him easier work and make him conquer it on his own, and then rebuild his confidence by praising him when he succeeds. If the worker is suffering from unjustified feelings of insignificance, the manager can show his true opinion of the worker's ability by praising him or by placing him in an important post. If the worker is suffering from some private difficulties, the manager can counsel him and help him through. If the worker has a serious psychological condition, the manager should recommend that he seek professional help.

The manager should take these steps, watch for their results, and continue to take whatever steps may be necessary.

When a Worker is Discontented with His Position

Sometimes a worker is assigned a task which he feels is far below him. He may feel angry that his ability has been so underestimated and lose his positive attitude toward work. On the other hand, when a worker is assigned a task so great that he wonders if he is even capable of doing it, he feels that his manager trusts him. He faces the task positively and resolves to complete it no matter what.

This is an important lesson for managers in the process of deciding how to divide responsibilities. Each worker should be assigned a job that is slightly beyond his ability.

I recall an episode that took place in Shitaya, Tokyo.

> A new operator began working at the central telephone office. She had the most severe physical handicap of any telephone operator hired to that point. She pledged that she would work her hardest to set an example for generations to come and was even written up in the newspaper.
>
> A job that the average girl would hardly consider attractive was a great challenge to this young handicapped woman.

The only problem with this technique is when the gap between the worker's ability and the difficulty of the job is so great that he fears he can never do the job and loses his desire to try. This gap must always be carefully considered. To make sure that each of his workers is always trying to do a job that is slightly beyond his abilities, the manager must carefully observe the work each individual is doing. When workers have mastered their jobs, he must assign more challenging tasks or transfer them to new positions at which they are inexperienced. In the same way, he must lighten the workloads of any workers who are becoming buried in work that is too difficult for them.

The Joy of Achievement

A worker's will to work begins with his feeling that his job is interesting. When he finds his work interesting, he will put himself into it and become completely involved.

A worker finds his work interesting when he encounters a difficult problem, stretches his mental and physical abilities to solve it, and tastes the joy of achievement. The manager must guide his workers and help them face difficult problems, then provide the necessary support for them to solve the problems with their own power. The most important thing of all, however, is the way the manager responds when the worker succeeds in solving the problem.

The manager must share the joy of achievement with the worker; he must not neglect to praise the worker's efforts. With single projects, the results of the work should be studied and reflected upon as soon as the project is completed. Even with ongoing work, as each step of the job is completed the manager and the workers should look back over the progress of the work together.

The habit of sharing the joy of achievement makes work more interesting. It brings about the feeling of solidarity that comes from working together to accomplish something, and it deepens the relationship of mutual trust between manager and workers.

GROUP MOTIVATION

How does the motivation of an entire section differ from that of the individual? This is an important question for the manager.

Setting Attractive Group Objectives

When the manager sets an attractive objective for his workers, they become inspired to achieve it. They rise together to face the challenge and they attack the objective with their fullest energies. A basic problem, therefore, for anyone who hopes to manage is whether he can set objectives attractive enough for his group to respond in this way.

> *The Osaka branch of a major trading company was the problem branch: no matter who became president, it was perpetually in the red. When Mr. O.—through no desire of his own— was transferred and became president, he got a very negative impression of the internal workings of the branch. When he went out to greet the clients, he got an earful of complaints. It was a terrible start for him. Though it was a business office, workers came in late, internal administrative matters were in chaos, and there was a huge pile of bad debts from credit sales.*
>
> *After about three months, the new president had struggled back to his feet, and he announced a new three-year plan at a full staff meeting. His plan was to double sales over the next three years and to move the office from the present location, which was dreary and inconvenient, to the center of town.*
>
> *There was an amazing response to this announcement. Workers came in early, and meetings became lively. Workers and managers discussed work until late in the evening. Sales jumped dramatically. The three-year objective was achieved in a little over two years and the move was made to the new office.*
>
> *One evening when the entire company was out drinking together, a senior staff member told Mr. O. that the employees had been in a quandary since before he had come in as president. They were apprehensive about the losses: though they wanted to move to a new location, they felt they could never broach the subject as long as the branch was in the red. Mr. O. reminisced on his plan, saying it had succeeded by a fluke.*

What does everyone really want? If a manager can put his finger on the common hopes of the group and succeed in setting an attractive objective that will inspire them, the organization will explode with new energy and dramatic change will occur.

The best opportunity to set such an objective is when taking a new position. The crucial question is whether the manager has the insight to detect what the group is really yearning for in the early part of his assignment. There is usually something deep at work in the stagnated workplace which will not be readily apparent to the manager who makes only a perfunctory observation. His ingenuity and serious effort are demanded.

Some managers tend to set objectives that are a little too revolutionary. This is because the manager's viewpoint is different from that of his workers. But the true effectiveness of an objective depends on how well it brings together the efforts of the group. The manager must abandon hackneyed, conventional methods of setting objectives and act as a true leader of people, putting forth attractive objectives that will inspire everyone in his group to action.

SELF-CHECK

How attractive are the objectives you set?

☐ To tell the truth, there aren't even any clear objectives.

☐ To be perfectly honest, they may be attractive to me, but I don't think they're particularly attractive to the individual workers.

☐ They may not be as attractive as the one Mr. O. set, but since my staff participates fully in their planning, everyone works hard to achieve them.

☐ I can say that the objectives I set are attractive group objectives, based on a careful analysis of the actual desires of all involved.

Dividing Work for a Feeling of Accomplishment

The division of responsibilities at the workplace generally has a strong influence on the attractiveness of the work.

It is difficult for a person to take pleasure in his job with a horizontal division of responsibilities, in which his own function is only one very small part of the overall work process. A vertical division of responsibilities, however, in which a person can oversee his work through the planning and execution stages to the finished product, can lead to a feeling of accomplishment. The assembly line is a classic problem: if a worker does anything nonstandard, he will inconvenience the other workers; there is no room for innovation. To make matters more difficult, the finished product is no one person's achievement, but a conglomerate of everyone's efforts.

Figure 15. Horizontal and Vertical Division of Responsibilities

Horizontal

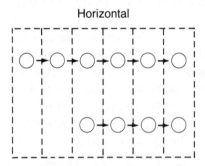

No room for innovation; hard to
see the results of own efforts;
"purity" of finished product is low.

Vertical

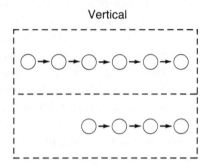

Room for innovation; results of
own efforts clearly visible; "purity"
of finished product is high.

Dividing work into units that are then completed as if they were jobs in themselves can bring a feeling of accomplishment lacking in long horizontal processes. For a corporation the ideal would be if each worker could prepare a balance sheet for his own performance. If it is too difficult to evaluate the results of one's efforts, work loses its game-like aspect and becomes unenjoyable.

In the service industries it often is possible for each individual worker to have his own balance sheet, and in manufacturing, income and expense figures or material quantities may be measured. It is in any case desirable to divide work so that each individual can measure his own performance.

Because this type of division of responsibilities makes the structure of different work functions much more complex, it requires a great deal of ability. Such alteration of work patterns can cause serious problems if not prepared for sufficiently. The manager must work up to it gradually, starting with a division of responsibilities that is not extremely complex and continuing from there.

Work becomes interesting to the degree that there is room for originality, the results of one's own effort are clearly visible, and the efforts of others do not affect one's own work. Managers must exercise their ingenuity to achieve a division of responsibilities that is attractive to their workers.

Supporting Small Group Activity

"Small group activity" refers to a technique in which workers are assigned to small groups, and the manager meets and talks with each group. Together they arrive at a working theme, analyze the causes of problems and devise countermeasures, and establish group objectives. The group then continues by working independently to reach these objectives. Members reflect on their performance and move on to establish new objectives.

Many different forms of small group activity are carried out on the organizational level. Some examples are the zero defects movement, quality control circles, the independent management movement, and various other groups within organizations. All of these belong to the concept of small group activity. They make work more interesting on the individual level by enhancing teamwork and bring new pleasure to the workplace.

The principle behind small group activity is that workers in large organizations often feel alienated because it is so difficult for them to perceive their individual contributions. When workers are placed in smaller groups, they can see how their own suggestions are realized and then directly connected to the finished product. They become more aware of the significance of their own existence in the organization. This method can be used in any type of organization, but it is particularly meaningful in the sort of workplaces mentioned earlier, where it is difficult to effect a division of responsibilities that will lead to a real feeling of accomplishment. Small group activity in such workplaces can do a great deal to bolster workers' will to work.

Regardless of the presence or absence of in-house small group activity in his organization, the manager can form and lead small groups on his own initiative, using the method as a powerful tool in motivating workers. This is part of one of the manager's most basic responsibilities—motivating people—so he must understand it well and work hard to put it to good use.

When companywide small group activity was first introduced, it was advanced as something in which managers did not participate. This was done originally to prevent old-school managers from interfering, but it led to a widespread lack of interest in small group activity on the part of managers. Yet the formation of small groups is in fact part of the managerial function of motivation—small group activity actually exists for the manager's sake! It gets nowhere without the participation of managers.

The major function of the manager in small group activity is to help the group get started and then to support it as it begins to succeed and to develop into a dynamic force in the workplace. He must not interfere with the group's internal workings, but he must be able to judge from the outside just how well the group is performing.

To this end, the manager must first express to the members of the group that he has deep concern and interest in their success. He must emphasize this point in front of the group from time to time, sit in on group meetings, and participate as a supportive element in all company activities. On the basis of his experience, he should present proposals on group formation or offer his opinions on improving existing groups. He should carefully examine any groups that are not performing well, locate the trouble spots, and give whatever guidance is necessary on objectives, methods, and leadership.

He must keep his mouth shut when it comes to the internal workings of the groups. The manager's key role in small group activity is to remove any obstacles that may exist and to make it easy for each group to perform its functions successfully.

Getting Away from the Role of Judge

There are many different types among the top administrators, directors, general managers, section managers, and operations managers of today's organizations, but one type that seems to exist at every level is the judge. The judge is seen very frequently in governmental offices and even to a certain degree in private corporations.

The judge is a manager who never offers his own ideas, but merely presides over his section, approving or disapproving proposals brought before him by his staff. He thinks his job is to look at his workers' reports and classify everything as either "yes," "no," or "pending." When he can't make a decision, things pile up on his desk until those under him lose all desire to work.

The judge never acts independently. His own opinions are not clear. He just sits at his desk, never moving around to persuade his superiors or colleagues, and never negotiating with those outside the organization. He does not rush in to help his workers either.

A totally passive manager like this will never inspire his workers. Managers must not be judges. Front-line managers in particular must be sure to join with their workers and become a central force to them.

Sometimes a manager is forced to take charge of a section that seems stagnant, a section in which no one seems to want to work.

This difficult situation is a telling indication of the manager's ability. One method is usually successful in such situations: the manager should make himself like the eye of a storm and then stir up the entire section with all his might. He must come in every morning long before everyone else and have meetings with the key people in the office before work starts. When he finishes these preparations and work hours begin, he starts the whirlwind going. He works at a furious pace, negating old ways of thinking and establishing new ones. He turns like a mighty engine until the entire section is set into motion.

At first the workers may be surprised and confused, or they may show resistance. If the manager keeps up a level of positive activity, however, the rest of the section will soon catch on. This is especially important for front-line managers.

As managers advance to higher administrative positions, they must continue to stir stagnant sections into action, but they must also survey the entire organization to learn the prevalent trends of each level. They must remove any obstacles that prevent those sections from doing their work. They must never be judges, getting a free ride from their workers. General managers must be especially alert to this danger.

The reform of the workplace atmosphere is a theme of perpetual importance in structural innovation.

SUMMARY OF CHAPTER 6

1. Motivation means stimulating the workers' desire to work and creating a workplace environment in which every worker is completely involved in his work. To achieve this goal, the manager must make both direct and indirect efforts. The essential point is that the manager must make his workers' jobs interesting.

2. All people have a natural will to work. The manager's effort to motivate workers consists of removing any individual obstacles that may be obstructing this will to work. The manager helps each worker to realize his own will to work normally.

3. The first thing a manager must do to motivate his workers is to examine himself for any bad habits that may be obstructing their will to work, and to correct these habits.

4. To motivate individuals, the manager must view them first in terms of their strong points and then praise these strong points openly. Everything starts from a positive approach to people.

5. The manager must teach his workers how to enjoy their work. This is especially important with new employees.

6. The manager must talk with problem workers, understand whatever personal problems they are struggling with, and help solve them.

7. The manager must understand all the undercurrents in his section, and be able to establish group objectives attractive enough to inspire everyone in the section to work. This is an important ability which determines the manager's value as a leader of people.

8. The manager must establish a system of work division that allows each worker to derive a feeling of accomplishment from his work. He must effectively support small group activity and get away from the judge role to become a central moving force to his workers. Reforming the workplace atmosphere is a theme of perpetual importance in structural innovation.

Chapter 7

Development

THE MEANING AND NATURE OF DEVELOPMENT

Changing the Workers

Development, put simply, means changing the workers. Three kinds of change may be involved.

First it is necessary to *correct any negative personality traits a worker may have*. In every section there are some workers who have not yet mastered the basics of being part of an organization. The first aspect of development is to correct this deficiency and to teach a new workplace lifestyle.

Workers of this sort are not trusted by their peers. Even if they have significant potential, they cannot realize it. One of the foremost responsibilities of the manager is to correct these bad habits. Anyone who cannot do this is unqualified for the position of manager.

There are many bad habits that a manager must correct: a worker may not work well; he may be incapable of teamwork; he may be habitually late; he may annoy others; he may neglect to report independently before he is asked.

The second aspect of development is *the enlargement of the worker's scope of abilities.* The manager must help each worker to do things he has never been able to do. He must make the workplace into an environment where each worker can gain new skills and expand the scope of his abilities continually.

131

There are many kinds of new skills. When a worker has more or less mastered his job, he can be taught to do a related job as well, or he can be transferred to a position for which he has absolutely no experience, where he will acquire new skills by conquering unfamiliar problems. A worker who has always worked alone can be taught to manage people himself. In a word, the second aspect of development is to make workers capable of doing things they have never done before.

The third aspect of development is *actually changing the way a worker thinks*. This can be done in many different ways. A worker who has never thought of anything other than keeping his own work in order can be encouraged to think of the entire office. A worker who never paid much attention to what others say can be turned into a good listener. A worker who was never able to put his thoughts in order can be developed into a rational, logical thinker. A worker who was never good at adjusting his own views when circumstances changed can be made into a sensitive and observant person. There are many different changes that can be made.

Development consists of correcting bad habits, teaching new skills, and changing old ways of thinking. These are all essentially ways of bringing about new states of mind in workers. Development means more than simply wishing a worker would do this or do that. In essence, it requires the alteration of people's personality traits and the expansion of their abilities. Every manager must learn how to bring about this kind of change in people.

The word *development* has long had a vague and somewhat romantic sound to it. But development is a very concrete thing. It means bringing about a new condition in the mind of the worker. Certainly it is difficult to measure the results of development quantitatively; its nature is very subjective. Nonetheless, one cannot consider development an abstract concept.

SELF-CHECK

How is your performance with the kind of development discussed above?

☐ Unfortunately, it's not so good.

☐ I am confident that I have done very well so far at changing people.

☐ I do well on the whole, but with some people I just have to give up.

The Objective of Development

The manager's objective in developing his workers is to fulfill his responsibility toward their lives. The manager must never pass his own bad habits on to his workers. He must never rob them of their ability to think independently by forcing too much instruction on them. His foremost responsibility is to make the best possible use of his short time with his workers to develop their abilities.

Some managers "develop" workers to serve their own interests. There are many variations of this false development, from the manager who is not even aware of what he is doing and acts out of the simple desire to control others, to the manager who deliberately forms a clique of toadies to increase his own power. But the thinking behind these forms of "development" is fundamentally wrong. In each case the manager will eventually lose the trust of his staff, his superiors, and his colleagues.

A manager does not sell new abilities to his workers in return for loyalty or service, acting simply out of a desire to control others. Rather, a manager develops his workers so that each of them can grow, win the trust of his peers, and derive satisfaction from his job. A worker developed in this way will most likely be grateful to his manager and perhaps come to trust him, but this is by no means the objective of development. It is merely a result of development, and one that the manager must never take advantage of.

Both the technique of development and the spirit behind it are important. No matter how skilled a manager's technique may be, if he does not have the proper spirit nothing will come of his efforts.

Every manager must remember that development is something he does for the sake of the workers, not for his own sake.

Mr. H. was a very average sort of fellow until the day he became a section manager, but a few years after his promotion, he was assigned to the top position in a new enterprise designed to play the decisive role in reversing a downward trend in the sales of the company's major product. He played the leading part in this new enterprise until it was well established; he had the reputation of being not only an expert salesman, but also an ex-

cellent developer of people. A number of people found their lives completely changed by working with him for a few years. He would have become the executive director of the new business, but instead of advancing through the ranks of higher management, he left for a job as an executive of a small company, retiring some years thereafter. Years later, I had the opportunity to chat about old times with the man who had been president of Mr. H.'s company at the time.

"Mr. H. was a sharp businessman—he had ability and wisdom. But he had a problem when it came to developing workers. He was very good to people who went along with him, but he was cold to anyone who didn't. He played favorites with workers. He gave power to people who listened to him, but the way he dealt with anyone who wanted to leave his section for another was downright inappropriate. He was a capable man and I was sorry to see him go, but anyone as egotistic as that can never succeed in higher management."

Believe in the Workers' Potential

The most important element of the manager's attitude toward his workers and their development is that he believe in their potential.

Every manager supervises some workers who lack ability, but he must never decide that they are hopeless and give up on developing them. The manager must rid himself of all prejudice and believe in every worker's potential for change and growth, regardless of sex, age, or employment status.

Any worker can be developed if his manager is determined and makes the necessary effort. True, organizations include all kinds of people, each with his own idiosyncrasies and personality traits. But all too often a manager makes a negative judgment about a certain individual and makes no further effort to develop him. This judgment is merely a justification for his own lack of experience at changing people, and his consequent feeling of powerlessness.

The manager must believe in his workers' potential. This is the first step of development.

At a local branch of a certain bank, there was a woman employee who was single and over 30. She worked in the general af-

fairs section, where she was known as having a mean streak—once she even reduced a new girl to tears. The section manager received frequent complaints about her.

When a new branch manager came in and was learning about the branch, he heard of this woman. Since she had entered the bank, she had been rotated from position to position within the branch just like the other young women, but wherever she went she had a terrible reputation for her nasty temper. She had been warned countless times, but the more she was approached the more obstinate she became. Finally she had been deposited in the general affairs section, which was run by older workers.

The new branch manager met with her and talked with her, and after considering a number of alternatives, he decided to place her in the window services section, the bank's most important section, which until then had been staffed entirely by male workers. There was a negative reaction from the bank's higher administrators but he squelched it and, telling the acting branch manager to reconcile himself to his lot, ordered the unusual personnel change.

The employee herself was nonplussed, but to everyone's surprise she adjusted completely to the change within a month's time. She lost her brusqueness, faced her job with new effort and concentration, finished her work every day with speed and precision, and showed powers of judgment that were on a par with those of her male predecessor. Perhaps because she had gained new confidence, she even became friendly with the younger women in the bank and quickly erased her bad reputation.

Managerial Agriculture

Development means changing workers. The manager does not force people to become what he wants them to be, but he creates an atmosphere in which it is easy for his workers to make the changes they need to make naturally.

In the American management technique known as MDP (Management Development Program), the qualifications for various managerial positions are elucidated and a number of candidates are nominated for each post. Each candidate's qualifications are closely scrutinized and compared with the qualifications for the position being considered. The candidates are then trained to supplement any deficiencies discovered.

This technique looks at the human being almost as a defective part, which is then repaired through training and assembled with other parts into a finished product. But a human being is not a part—a human being is a living thing capable of growing and developing its own abilities independently.

Development supports each individual's natural ability to grow; it means removing obstacles to allow the individual to stretch his own ability to the limit. Development is different from the mechanical approach of MDP. The concept of development is organic. The manager cultivates the soil and waters the seeds until sprouts come up; he protects the young plants from wind and straightens them when they bend. Finally, he transforms the saplings into strong trees by exposing them to wind and rain, and they continue to grow through their own natural vitality.

The "hard" approach to development is no longer valid in today's changing organizational environments. Even if a manager attempts to set certain working conditions and force his workers to adjust themselves accordingly, the conditions themselves will change before long. Development is an organic concept; the manager must take time and exercise diligence to let all his workers grow.

I do not wish to negate every element of MDP. The technique contains many valuable tips for Japan, where job descriptions are so ambiguous.

New Challenges

Development means establishing conditions in the workplace that make it easy for workers to change and grow. One of the best methods of development is to place a worker in a position for which he has no experience, where he will face new challenges, conquer them, and gain confidence. A worker grows during the process of confronting a new challenge, straining himself, and ultimately conquering it. At the same time he gains confidence and acquires new abilities that both he and his peers will recognize.

There are three different methods of initiating this process. The first is to examine the ability levels of the workers in their present positions and to add new tasks to their jobs before they become routine and unchallenging. The second is to raise the overall ability level of the section by periodically rotating every worker to a new position for which he has no experience. The third method is to transfer workers who have already been developed to a certain ability level, assigning them to new positions in other sections, and giving them new opportunities to grow.

Several elements in the timing of rotation and transfer require caution. One is the issue of whether the worker in question has progressed sufficiently in his "education" at his present job to have the confidence that will be demanded of him in his new position. A worker who is transferred before he has mastered his own job will never gain confidence. It does him no good to keep getting kicked upstairs.

The timing of transfers is very important; they must come neither too soon nor too late. If the transfer is made too soon, the worker will have been kicked upstairs and will not master his new job. On the other hand, the worker should not be kept in the same position forever. The manager must accurately gauge the timing of transfers to ensure the success of the workplace.

Managers who dislike the idea of transferring an experienced worker to another section because it will mean an increase in their own workloads are even less qualified to manage than those whose timing is poor. It is certainly difficult to send an able worker to another section, but it is the manager's responsibility to back up the experienced worker's successor, to guide him, and to develop him into a competent member of the section. To shirk this responsibility and sit idly by while an experienced worker takes care of things is not only selfish, but it undermines the overall quality of the workers themselves.

A manager shows his true spirit by working hard to train people and then sending these trained, capable people to other sections. At the same time, he welcomes new and inexperienced people, and does his best to help them change and grow.

The Manager as an Example

The first thing a manager must think about as he approaches the subject of development is whether he himself has any negative characteristics that might adversely affect his workers. If he finds that he does, he must take the necessary steps to correct them.

There are managers everywhere who do not develop their workers properly. Some spell out every instruction to the letter and leave the workers no room to think on their own, making them into passive people and choking their powers of thought. Some keep their workers in the same positions for too long, preventing the development of the other workers. Some overlook workers' bad habits, which they should be correcting. Some fail to motivate their workers and end up making them lose their will to work or allowing their interest to be diverted. The examples go on and on. In every case, the manager creates an extremely grave problem by lowering the quality of his staff. A manager who finds that he has committed any of these errors must take immediate steps to reform himself completely.

Workers tend unconsciously to imitate their superiors. This tendency is particularly strong in Japan, where most managerial positions are occupied by older, experienced people. Workers observe their managers' daily actions very closely, although at a glance they may not seem to be doing so. Though they do imitate their managers' good points, they also imitate their more undesirable points, assuming that if the manager does it, they can do it too. Workers learn from whatever the manager shows them. If a manager hopes to develop his staff into a hard-working, successful group, he must show them what he expects by being an example to them himself. It is not only illogical but totally ineffective to tell your workers, "Don't do what I do—just do what I say."

> *Years ago, there was a popular photo of a father, sprawled half asleep in front of the television set, being scolded by his child, "Do your homework!" The folly of "do as I say, not as I do" is the same in the workplace as it is at home.*

SELF-CHECK

Is there any part of you that it would be dangerous for your workers to imitate?

☐ I don't think so.

☐ Perhaps there is. I need to reevaluate the way I go about my daily activities.

☐ My staff does what they want, and I do what I want.

Work as Development

For the manager, doing his job means developing people, and developing people means doing his job. By development, I do not mean the actual education of the worker somewhere outside of the workplace. I am referring to the manager's function of making the workplace an environment where each worker can naturally grow and acquire new skills.

This should be clear from the example of assigning workers to jobs for which they have no previous experience. It is part of the manager's routine work to assign tasks and functions to his workers, but the real issue is how well he can ensure their development as he does this.

This, in essence, is the manager's job. If his delegation of responsibilities is skillful, his workers will grow; if the delegation is ill considered, they will not. This is why workers seem to flourish and grow under some managers, whereas under other managers ten years of experience might as well have been a single day, and the workers grow only in age. The manager must give careful consideration to the development aspect of every task he assigns.

The question of how to do on-the-job training is perhaps the stupidest question of all time. All training is essentially "on the job." It is through their contact with their peers and managers in the workplace that workers grow. The manager's job is to develop his workers; "development" for him means working together with his workers.

The question is, how much of an educational effect does the manager have in his relationship with his workers? In every moment he passes with them, to what degree does he base his words and actions on education? This is the difference between a novice manager and a seasoned manager.

Work as an Educational Medium

Suppose a manager has told one of his workers to come up with a plan to deal with a certain problem, and that worker has drafted the plan and delivered it. Unfortunately, however, the plan is full of holes and requires a considerable amount of reworking. What does the manager do? Here are two examples:

A. *The cleanup type* indicates and explains specifically, in detail, each part of the plan that needs to be rethought, added to, or subtracted from. He tells the worker to fix the plan and resubmit it immediately.

B. *The development type* first considers how soon the plan is needed. If it is needed by noon the next day, he tells the worker what is wrong with the plan and has him write it up again for submission and discussion the next morning.

Although either method will get the job done in time, method A cleans up the plan faster. Unfortunately, however, the job then cannot serve as an educational medium for the worker. Method B not only accomplishes the job but allows it to serve as a medium for the maximum development of the worker's abilities. With method B, "work" and "education" are one and the same.

It is not enough that work gets done, as with method A. The manager must make every job an opportunity for the worker to think; he must use the job as an educational tool so the worker who does it can learn from it. Managers who are skilled at developing people do this automatically at every opportunity.

A manager sees his workers every day, giving instructions, receiving reports, and consulting with them. His everyday discussions with them may seem casual, but the cumulative effect of these exchanges over the years is profound. If the manager is the cleanup type, his words will be of no use to his workers and he will stunt their development. If he is the development type, however, and uses every assignment as an educational tool, his workers will grow and progress in leaps and bounds.

Before a manager can use every assignment as an educational tool, he must think far into the future and make sure that he has the necessary leeway. This has nothing to do with how busy the manager is—it has more to do with whether he is doing his job systematically. If a manager gets so far behind in his work that every operation in his section is running late, the cleanup style of management will become his only alternative.

Patience and Perseverance

Patience and perseverance are of the utmost importance in any effort to develop workers. Impatience is anathema in such efforts—

remember that development is like farming.

People are not easily changed, and opportunities to change them are rare. Change is usually so slow and gradual that it is not apparent, even to the individual who is changing.

Some managers get angry when they see no change after warning a worker about a bad habit; they decide the worker is no good. But this sort of labeling is an extremely serious error. A person's lifestyle is not so easily changed. A manager need merely look at himself to see this.

In such a situation, the manager must never get angry. He must simply repeat the warning calmly, over and over again, until the worker is cured of his bad habit. Development always takes time. If the manager maintains his efforts from day to day, the signs of change will begin to show gradually. After a certain period of time he will look back and realize that the worker has changed significantly. Patience and perseverance is the essential theme of development.

DEVELOPING NEW EMPLOYEES

Developing by "Show-and-Tell"

The proper approach to development depends on the position of the worker and the stage of growth he has already attained. For the new employee, who has yet to become a functioning member of the organization, the "show-and-tell" method is most appropriate. The best way to develop new employees who know nothing about the job is to teach them the methods that experience has proven to be the best. This is done in the following order:

1. A senior worker performs the task while explaining it to the new worker, responding to the new worker's questions.

2. The new worker tries to perform the task himself.

3. The senior worker comments on the new worker's performance.

4. Steps (2) and (3) are repeated.

The standard method is for the senior worker to take the new worker by the hand and show him how the job is done. This is the exact reverse of simply giving the new worker a job and expecting him to learn it himself. Managers who use that approach would be shirking their responsibilities. Because the new employee has no knowledge whatsoever, it is both inefficient and ineffective to make him learn a job himself with no models and no guidance. He will gain no confidence, and he will become anxious. The best approach is to teach the new worker the best time-proven methods, so that at the very least he will be able to start off on the right foot at his new position.

It is common to establish a one-to-one individual guidance system through which each new worker can be trained for a set period by a worker several years his senior. This method not only educates the new worker and develops the senior worker assigned to him, but ensures a thorough development of new employees by involving more of the workplace in the effort.

> *There is a well-known song that was popularized by Admiral Isoroku Yamamoto, commander-in-chief of the Combined Fleet of Japan during World War II:*

> > *"Show them how to do it,*
> > *tell them and ask them, make them do it,*
> > *praise them, or else they'll never learn!"*

Learning How to Enjoy Work

New employees usually receive an overall introduction to their organization before being assigned to a specific section or department. The managers receive these new employees and help them adjust to their new work environment. The new employees are then taught to master one job after another, gaining confidence as they learn.

The manager should set a schedule for the education of new workers, decide which jobs the new worker should be taught during each period, and assign each new worker to a senior employee for training. The new worker's on-the-job training should begin with his mastery of the basic techniques and end with his experiencing the more independent aspects of work: devising new methods, thinking of ways to improve the present techniques, and submitting plans and proposals to his manager. In this way, the manager should carefully think out, establish, and achieve new worker development objectives.

The development of new employees means more than just teaching them their new jobs. They must be taught how to think and plan improvements, and how to enjoy their work. This is an extremely important point: if a worker learns these arts early in his career, he will be much easier to motivate later on.

The same basic approach should be taken with workers who are not new to the company, but who have been transferred to a position with which they have no experience. These workers too should be taught by the show-and-tell method. Thorough training should never be neglected in deference to the worker's pride, as this will only hurt the worker later on.

Basic Training

Every new worker must undergo basic training so that he will know how he is expected to behave in his organization.

There is no one authoritative set of rules for the basic training of new workers, but some elements that experience has proven important are listed below:

Confirm instructions: When a worker receives instructions, he must ask questions about any part of them he does not understand, repeating the instructions back to his manager if necessary so he can carry them out accurately.

Report on actions: When a worker has carried out some instructions he has received, he must go on his own, before being asked, to the person who gave them to him and report on his actions.

Communicate precisely: All communication within the section and outside it must be made with precision and speed; the worker must never inconvenience others with inaccurate or tardy communication.

Speed up bad reports: When there is an accident or a complaint, it must be reported immediately so that necessary countermeasures are not delayed.

Observe work hours and deadlines strictly: A worker must never inconvenience others by failing to be prompt for work, conferences, and other workplace functions, or by failing to meet deadlines in his own work.

Write clearly and carefully: Workers must prepare all memos, reports, and other documents clearly and legibly.

Report concisely: Just as with written reports and documents, verbal reports, telephone conversations, and other communication should be concise and accurate.

Cooperate spontaneously: Members of groups must help one another, automatically coming to the aid of other workers who are overly busy or are having difficulty with their work.

Have appropriate attire and manners: Personal attire should be appropriate to the workplace. Workers must use decent speech and manners so as not to make others uncomfortable or cause misunderstandings.

Respond quickly: Workers must respond and act quickly when they are asked questions or given instructions.

Have precise working habits: Workers must always be on time for work; they must never be late or absent without permission or a proper reason.

Separate company and private matters: Workers must not use the company phone for personal calls or take office supplies for their own use. They must not use company time or company employees for their personal business.

Be sensitive to the needs of other employees: Workers should never talk about their colleagues behind their backs; male workers must never make indiscreet remarks to their female co-workers. Workers must not have any bad habits that will make their co-workers uncomfortable.

General: Workers must make speedy and effective efforts to remove any elements that might make others uncomfortable or work more difficult.

The essence of basic training is that it makes the workplace an easier place for others to work. It is most effective to begin a worker's basic training immediately after his entry into the organization. In the years to come, it will become increasingly difficult to correct his bad habits. Any senior worker who has yet to master his basic training will earn the mistrust and stunt the growth of his co-workers.

The manager must make repeated and tenacious efforts to see

that all new employees graduate from their basic training. He should correct their bad habits or warn them about mistakes one at a time. Only when they have finally stopped repeating one mistake should he begin to warn them about the next.

SELF-CHECK

☐ It would be hard for me to say that I have been sufficiently persistent in my workers' basic training as described above.

☐ I guess I'm training my workers pretty well, but there is a part of me that seems to miss certain points and give up on others.

☐ I persevere and guide my workers quite sufficiently on all the important points. The workers I put through basic training graduate with honors.

The key to the development of new workers is the show-and-tell method. This method consists of allowing workers to gain confidence quickly, putting them through basic training so they master the skills of being part of an organization, and building and firm foundation of mutual trust.

The manager must keep in constant contact with his new employees, taking every opportunity to observe them and consult with them, to hear their thoughts and opinions freely, to answer their questions, and to let them have their say. These techniques are useful not only in the actual training of new employees, but also as a means for the manager to become familiar with and understand the thoughts and feelings of the new generation of workers.

A manager's new workers are the leading indicator of the future of the organization to which he belongs.

DEVELOPING EXPERIENCED WORKERS

Remedial Education

To develop experienced workers, the manager must examine

them carefully to make sure they have graduated successfully from their basic training, supplementing their skills with any remedial education that proves necessary. Even if a manager is completely confident that all the workers he put through basic training are competent, he will frequently discover that experienced workers transferred from other sections require some remedial education.

Just as with new employees, the show-and-tell method must be used. Even experienced workers need to be shown and explained to repeatedly until they master the basics. The manager must not hesitate to correct the flaws in the basic training of experienced workers, as these flaws will ultimately undermine their self-confidence and retard their future growth. With experienced workers, however, it is especially important that the manager explain carefully what the worker is doing wrong and why it is wrong, and that the worker himself be convinced. The experienced worker has his pride and his reputation among the other workers to think about, so the manager must be careful not to cause him to lose face.

Mr. E. was thirty-five years old and a graduate of Tokyo University. He had been with the company for twelve years and was promoted to assistant section manager of the survey section.

But about a month after Mr. E. assumed his new post, the manager of the section began to have serious misgivings. Mr. E. seemed unable to prepare even simple proposals and reports on time. If the section manager reminded him or hurried him, his pride was hurt and he became disgruntled.

At first, the section manager assumed that Mr. E. was still unused to his new position, but three months passed and six months passed and his performance was still unacceptable. What was worse, the documents he did prepare were of insufficient quality. The section manager was at his wit's end.

One day, the section manager corrected the draft of a circular that Mr. E. had prepared, handing it back to him completely covered with red marks. Mr. E. complained, and the section manager called him into a discussion room. The section manager explained very carefully to him that there were a lot of problems with his writing, and that until he "graduated" from this stage of the basics, his memos and drafts would be returned to him with corrections written in red. Mr. E. acquiesced.

As a result of the repetition of this process, Mr. E.'s writing did improve. With the help of his manager, he learned how to draft surveys and plans, and he made rapid progress. In fact, even the disgruntlement the section manager had seen at the beginning disappeared, and he began to work harmoniously with the other members of the section.

Later on, when the section manager became good friends with Mr. E., he learned that after his college graduation Mr. E. had, for personal reasons, worked in a small business where he was taught nothing, and that it was after a year of working there that he had entered his present company.

Three Things to Keep in Mind

Experienced workers often have three types of problems that are especially important to correct. The first is *overdependence on the manager,* typified by the worker who constantly asks, "What shall I do next?" The growth of such workers has been retarded by a serious deficiency in the ability to think originally. The manager must correct this deficiency immediately.

To do this, the manager must withhold the answer to the worker's question and instead ask, "What do you think you should do?" Even if the worker's suggestion is wrong, the manager should praise him and offer further guidance. When the worker realizes that if he approaches the manager he will only be asked to supply his own thought, he will move on from this stage.

The second problem is *defeatism.* The worker may approach the manager and say, "I can't." The "I can't" group poses a perpetual problem for the manager. He must teach them to think about the solutions that exist before they say they "can't." He must have discussions with them, give them hints, and offer them guidance. He must teach them how to find solutions.

The third kind of problem for the manager is the *unreceptive worker,* the one who thinks he knows everything and is unable to listen quietly to anyone else. It is easy for a worker to become this way when he makes steady progress in his work and racks up success after success. But since no matter how successful a person is, he can ensure his future growth only by listening to what others have to say, this type of worker often stops developing and all of his talents become buried.

To deal with the unreceptive type, the manager must assign more difficult tasks and make him struggle with them. At the same time, he may need to speak directly with the worker and encourage him. Workers sometimes become unreceptive because their managers praise them constantly, without occasionally slipping in a tough criticism. Excellent workers are not developed by praise alone.

Experienced workers are of central importance to the manager. He must give them his most thorough attention in all matters, and he must never miss an opportunity to guide them and correct them.

SELF-CHECK

Are there any "what shall I do next?," "I can't," and unreceptive types among your workers?

☐ Yes, there are.

☐ None.

☐ I'm not sure, but I'll think about it.

Developing by Entrusting

The main theme in the development of experienced workers is to entrust them with responsibility.

It is well known that workers learn by trial and error. When the manager entrusts work to them, he must leave plenty of room for this sort of growth. Workers develop a sense of responsibility for jobs entrusted to them; they learn by doing work that is new and unfamiliar to them.

But entrusting a worker with a job does not mean simply telling him to do the job however he likes. That would not be entrusting—it would be shirking the manager's responsibility for the guidance of his workers. Before entrusting a worker with a job, the manager must first make very clear how far along the worker should be with the job by what time. It is best if the manager can define these expectations by alternately approving or correcting proposals his workers submit to him, but if they do not come forward with any, he must direct them. He must at the very least make a clear decision on what the objectives of the job are.

The Japanese tend to like the gutsy approach: "Just do it!"
But this often leads to a confusion between the entrusting of

work to someone else and the shirking of one's own responsibility. Even Commander Iwao Oyama, known for his famous line, "Did you say there was a war going on somewhere?" during the Russo-Japanese war, had a clear objective—to win. A manager cannot shirk his leadership responsibility and get by on guts alone.

The essence of the "developing by entrusting" method may be summed up as follows:

1. Set a goal.

2. Leave the method up to the worker.

3. Back up his efforts and help him to succeed.

The key to developing by entrusting is in methodology. This is what speeds worker growth. In some cases, backup work is unnecessary; in others a considerable degree is required. In either case, the experienced worker must be helped to succeed and thereby made to build up his own self-confidence, just as described in the earlier discussion on building the work environment.

Entrustment and Timing

The inexperienced manager may encounter problems in entrusting workers with jobs. No matter how well he sets objectives for his workers and leads them to think about methods of doing the job, they may take so long that it is not ready in time.

Many managers in this situation end up simply telling the worker how to do the job. But even if the worker does the job as he is told and succeeds at it, instead of gaining new abilities he may end up getting an inferiority complex. Some workers may even extract from this experience the false lesson that it's always best just to ask the manager how. They may give up on original thinking and lapse into a state of depending on their manager for everything.

The manager must achieve a delicate balance between the entrustment of workers with jobs and the deadlines those jobs may have. To do this, he must observe his workers carefully, gauge their abilities, and allow them enough leeway to do the job and grow in the process without having to drive themselves to the brink of exhaustion. This technique is one of the key skills of the experienced manager.

The manager must do his best to avoid situations in which he himself is surprised by a deadline and must drop everything to clean up at the last minute. This sort of crisis frustrates the workers and is very rarely a positive experience.

The manager must make each of his workers cross a mountain, and when they have crossed it, he must make them cross another. He must give them his continued, scrupulous attention and never be impatient. Developing a worker is like polishing a jewel: it requires a sustained expenditure of time and effort.

SELF-CHECK

Comment on your own style of entrustment:

☐ To tell the truth, I have my hands full with just getting the work done. I have not progressed to the point where I can set objectives for my workers and leave the actual methods up to them.

☐ Well, it's okay, but I couldn't say that I set objectives properly every time I entrust a job to someone.

☐ I have mastered the art of developing by entrusting.

DEVELOPING KEY PERSONS AND MANAGERS

This section deals with the development of persons who hold positions of responsibility within the organization. The problems discussed are encountered in the development of chief clerks and supervisors by section managers, or in the development of section managers by general managers.

Training for Management

The development of supervisors, foremen, chiefs, group leaders—in short, those in lower management positions who have people working under them—can be divided into two stages. The first stage begins when the employee assumes his new position and ends when he is completely familiar and experienced with his function. In general, this period is longer in workplaces where there is frequent change; it is relatively short in a stable, unchanging workplace. It is during this first stage that the employee masters maintenance management.

The second stage is the preparation stage, during which the employee is prepared to become a key person or a manager. The employee must be guided in the basics of management during this period.

Carefully examine the employees to see if they have any selfish thoughts, or if they have the proper compassion for those under them. Do they help workers who are in trouble, and have they set up systems to train new workers? How well have they managed to balance their concerns for the occupational side and the human side of work?

Since many of these people will have worked for long years as specialists in one field or another, they may not necessarily have a good sense of the balance between the work itself and the people who do it. This and other essential parts of management ability must be carefully observed, and any necessary advice or guidance offered.

The relationship of mutual trust between these people and those under them also bears careful observation. Their future success as managers will depend on whether they can inspire their workers with a feeling of solidarity.

Employees who look like specialist material must be made to research their specialties with unequaled depth. The content of their research must not be merely academic: they must be well versed in practical problems and issues that will later qualify them to lead structural innovations. In many cases, specialists need to have more persuasive power than managers; their ability to prepare and give presentations is especially important.

Because the two positions have so much in common, it is often difficult to judge whether an employee should be developed as a manager or as a specialist, but the guidance effort is extremely important in either case.

Guiding with Objectives

The principle of developing key persons and managers is the same as that of developing experienced workers: develop by entrusting. The developer must establish objectives clearly, lead the individual to think about the methods he will use, and then step in to offer any necessary backup support.

But in this stage, the autonomy of the individual being developed must be polished. When developing an experienced worker, the developer has no choice but to set the objectives himself, but in the development of employees for management positions, it is important to explain to the employee that he must take this burden upon himself. It is essential to develop in him the habits of examining current problems himself, devising objectives on his own, and approaching his superiors to discuss whatever plans he has prepared.

At this point, the developer meets with the employee being developed, discusses his plan, and either approves it or changes it. Less guidance and backup are offered than with regular employees; the central element of this sort of development is to bring about a situation in which there is no doubt that the employee being developed will think and act on his own accord.

Teach the employee to think "one level higher." From this viewpoint, have him master the technique of devising various plans for the area of which he will take charge. An employee should actually be taught to think like an executive from the time he becomes a supervisor.

Workload Adjustment

After the training described above, the next consideration in the development of key persons and executives is the adjustment of their individual workloads.

These employees are of an age at which they are most active; they are at their physical primes and can stand hard work, and their ability to change is at its peak. The most capable of them, therefore, must stretch their abilities dramatically, and those who are less capable must be endowed with more skill and self-confidence.

The best way to do this is to assign a large amount of new and unfamiliar work to those who are handling their present jobs with ease, thereby forcing them to conquer new difficulties and grow in the process. They may be asked to fill in for a section manager or called on for negotiations within the organization or outside. The most promising employees should be loaded down with more and more trials and made to "graduate" from each of them one at a time.

With employees who do not perform as they should, identify the cause of the failure. If it lies in a lack of ability, lighten the workload and guide them until they have it completely mastered. If this works, pile on the work again, and if they falter again, lighten the load yet another time. With this kind of guidance, employees with potential abilities will grow quickly, and less able employees will naturally find their proper places.

The workload adjustment approach is effective for people in higher levels of management as well.

Development of Managers by General Managers

The first trial a general manager, plant manager, or branch manager must face in the development of his staff managers is whether he can influence and change a section manager.

The major function of the general manager class in an organization is to carry out structural innovations. This class is not concerned with maintenance management. A general manager is therefore not doing his job if he merely sits on the heads of his section managers, acting as a communications link between them and the president and busying himself with routine work.

The general manager's efforts to develop his managers must be more active than this. He must constantly introduce them to new ideas and ways of thinking, making the section boil like a crucible. He must bring about dramatic increases in the abilities of his section managers by making them aim for higher goals, guiding them to meet these objectives, and adjusting their workloads appropriately up and down.

The general manager must be able to judge which stage the managers under him are in—imperfect maintenance management, maintenance management, passive structural innovation, or active structural innovation—and take whatever steps are necessary to advance them. If the stage of imperfect maintenance management continues for more than one year after a manager assumes a new position, the general manager must correct this. He must clearly tell managers who are capable only of maintenance management that their abilities are insufficient, teaching them himself about structural innovation and bringing them at least to the level where they can participate passively. After a certain period of time at this level, the managers must be brought to suggest their own themes for structural innovation. The general manager must guide them and prompt them again and again until they become capable of active structural innovation.

The objective of the general manager is to develop every manager, except those who were left behind at the stage of imperfect maintenance management, and to bring them all to the stage of active structural innovation. In this way, he will ensure that the efforts of his managers always lead directly to progress.

Unfortunately, the general manager must also exercise his ingenuity to find places for those managers who were never quite able to advance beyond the maintenance management stages and to keep them occupied until they leave their posts. And he must be especially vigilant of the workers underneath these managers, making sure that they mature in their jobs.

The general manager's duty is to keep the managers under him growing and changing, even after their youth is far behind them.

SUMMARY OF CHAPTER 7

1. Development means changing workers, and has three major themes: correcting their bad habits, endowing them with new abilities, and revolutionizing their ways of thinking.

2. Remember always that development must be done purely for the sake of the workers, and never for the sake of the manager. A manager who tries to develop workers for selfish purposes will in the end earn their mistrust.

3. The manager must have faith in his workers' potential to change. He must never judge people. This is the first step of development.

4. Developing a person means creating an environment in which the seeds of his abilities will naturally come to life. Like farming, it requires persistent effort over a long period of time. The manager must never try to develop workers by forcing them into a mold that he himself has created.

5. When a person faces a new and unfamiliar problem, struggles with all his might, and succeeds in conquering it, he gains self-confidence and new abilities that will be apparent both to himself and to others.

6. In developing his workers, the first thing the manager must do is make a conscious effort to correct any bad habits he may have, before he ends up damaging the workers. He must be a model to them in every respect.

7. Work is development. Development takes place as the manager and his staff work together. The manager must plan his workers' activities to afford them the maximum of opportunities for development. Work is all: the manager must always make sure that every job he assigns serves as an educational medium.

8. The "show-and-tell" method should be used in the development of new employees. In the earliest stage of his career, the new employee must completely master the basics of working as part of an organization.

9. In the development of experienced employees, the first order is remedial education in the basics. The "what next?" type, the "I can't" type, and the unreceptive type must each be completely restored to health. Using the "developing by entrusting" method, the manager must then set objectives for them, leave the methods up to them, and step in with any backup support necessary to help them to success.

10. In the development of key persons and managers, the degree to which they have mastered the basics of management must be determined and the necessary guidance offered. It is important that they be taught with objectives, and in particular that they become skilled at setting their own objectives autonomously. Using "workload adjustment," stretch the abilities of the more capable employees and allow the less capable ones to find their own levels.

11. The main responsibility of the general manager class is structural innovation. General managers must therefore examine the managers under them and evaluate their present ability levels. They must work with the objective of eventually developing all the managers under them to the stage of active structural innovation. The general manager's duty is to keep the managers under him growing and changing, even after their youth is far behind them.

CONCLUSION

Manager, Revolutionize Thyself!

As we have seen, today's manager begins his career by mastering maintenance management and then moves on to influence his workers, superiors, and colleagues while he initiates and leads structural innovations. With every new position he assumes, he leaves lasting proof that he has lived and functioned as a member of his organization. He does this by building up a store of "permanent assets" that constitute some sort of lasting contribution to his organization; by creating an attractive workplace for his workers in which each individual is completely involved with his job and all are bound together in a relationship of mutual trust; and by changing the lives of his workers.

The ideals are high and the road is long and hard, but the manager must first examine himself coolly to discover any failings, conquer them one by one, and carry on a continuous revolution within himself.

The worth of today's manager is not determined by the absolute value of his present abilities, but rather by his potential for growth and change in the future. Even a manager who is at a very high level is worthless if he remains stagnant, whereas a manager with flexibility and large growth potential is worth a great deal to his organization. The most important theme for managers living in today's changing times is self-reform.

Believe In Change

When we are young and inexperienced, we feel that we have un-limited potential. All too often, as we begin to acquire experience, en-dure the hardships of work, and advance in years, we begin to see our limits and make less and less effort to change and reform ourselves.

The manager, however, whether he perceives it or not, changes over the long term. If he continues to make a serious effort within his environment, he can expect to change considerably.

The manager must take pleasure in assuming a new post. Every new position, and particularly one for which he has no experience, is a golden opportunity for self-reform. He must adopt a positive out-look and make the most of these opportunities to develop himself. If he approaches these opportunities negatively and stints in his efforts, the results will be unfortunate for both him and his organization.

When a manager feels that he has been in the same position for too long and that his present job is becoming routine, he can set new objectives for himself, strive to meet them, and experience the same sort of self-reform he would have undergone had he assumed an en-tirely new position. When we strive for extremely high objectives, we are necessarily pushed to make new efforts and find revolutionary methods.

Merely following this empirical approach, however, the man-ager is bound to run into trouble. There are two dangers he may en-counter. The first is that the cycle of entering a new and unfamiliar job, conquering the challenge, and growing through his success may make him overconfident and he may lose his malleability. In other words, a person may stop growing when he begins to believe that his own way of doing things is always right.

The second pitfall is that before he realizes it, the manager's field of vision may narrow and his receptivity to changes in the times or in the organizational or external environments may become dulled. It is not unusual for a person who is repeatedly successful to grow so en-thusiastic about his work that he loses sight of all else and becomes the equivalent of an *idiot savant*.

An Independent Development Program

To protect himself from the dangers described above, the man-ager must devise for himself an ongoing development program that will stimulate him from many different angles and keep him informed. He must read widely, take correspondence courses, and attend seminars both inside and outside the company. He must attend conventions, trade fairs, and nationwide meetings of groups connected with his field, and he must associate with people in other fields.

As they grow older, managers tend more and more to simply pick up knowledge; they devote less and less time to actual study. They rely more heavily on intuitive responses, and their ability to think logically weakens. It is very important, however, to develop the habit of stopping from time to time to take a close look at things. This is what the printed word is for.

The manager does not read magazines and newspapers in the hope of memorizing their contents. He reads, rather, so that he may think about what is said, make analogical inferences, understand ideals that are unlike his own, and create his own ideas. In this way, a manager can glean some information from the printed word and then, through the reasoning process, arrive at a new idea or method. The mere accumulation of knowledge is meaningless. It is quite sufficient for a manager to know where he can find something, so that when he needs it he can get it. The real issue is what he can do with knowledge or information once he acquires it.

Books and the views of others enrich one's own knowledge. They are the catalytic agents in the planning of one's own actions, and they must be used independently. It is especially important for a manager to have his own ideas. He must therefore use these catalytic agents to raise his intellectual potential. He must expose himself to views that are either in agreement or disagreement with his own, and that will lead him, by the reasoning process, to new and original ideas.

Friends and Advisors

Managers sometimes encounter situations they cannot judge or problems they cannot solve. Such situations or problems often become intense experiences that contribute to the individual's growth but are very painful.

In such times, it is very important that the manager have people he can talk to and ask advice of. Every manager must have at least one such person. That person does not necessarily need to be a business partner. It could just be a person who will sit with him and listen to his problems as a fellow human being.

The person could be a former teacher or a member of the clergy, a senior worker, or a former boss. As long as it is someone the manager has known and respected thus far, it could be anyone. When he feels stumped by something, he goes and talks. He may come to a decision during the course of the discussion, or just talk about what is vexing him. It is very important in life to have an advisor.

The manager's circle of friends is an important factor in determining his own level. If he has contacts with people who think on low levels or whose thinking is not constructive, his own thoughts will sink to a low level. On the other hand, if he associates with people who think on high levels, his own thoughts will naturally grow to higher and deeper levels.

This does not necessarily mean that the manager must associate only with those of high social standing. It means merely that if he has social contact with people whose attitudes are on high intellectual and spiritual levels, he will grow as a human being and his eyes will open.

Self-Evaluation

The final and most important issue in the self-reform of managers is their ability to evaluate coolly and accurately their abilities, strengths and weaknesses, and any traits or habits that may require correction. They need this ability to develop and improve themselves.

Managers are praised frequently for their successes and rarely criticized for their flaws. Thus they encounter the occupational hazard of responding innocently to this feedback by losing the ability to evaluate themselves accurately. This hazard grows more serious as the manager advances in rank and peaks at the executive level.

This is why humility is so important for the manager. He must have the ability to evaluate himself coolly and objectively, taking account of the biases present in the praise he receives.

The manager must value highly any "bitter-pill advice" he may be offered. Whether a manager has people around him who will speak frankly with him is a good indication of his character. If he is narrow-minded and hidebound, people will never be straight with him. The manager must therefore pay special attention to any criticism he receives and respond to it from within. Sometimes he must swallow the bitter pill.

The manager is also subject to the dangers of complacency. Using his position as a privilege will earn him the mistrust of those around him. The true fruition of management is to act independently according to one's beliefs and to aim for perfection as a human being, regardless of the surrounding conditions.

Health

The great prerequisite to all I have mentioned thus far is health. The job of manager is particularly stressful to the mind and the body, and paradoxically the work becomes more intense as the manager grows older. When the manager is out of sorts, the clear judgment on which his life depends may be obstructed. The manager must therefore train both his mind and his body, keeping himself in perfect health.

The manager matures as he grows older, becoming more skilled at judging others and at helping those he works with realize their fullest potential. He must reconcile many contradictory aspects of his job with one another. Only his accumulated experience will allow him to achieve these delicate balances.

It goes without saying that the manager must increase his own abilities and vision as he grows, aiming toward perfection as a human being. It is important for him to participate in social activities in his private life and to enrich himself by balancing his business and private lives appropriately. The manager must maintain a strong will to improve himself, even when he is old. He must add new ideas and new abilities day by day, year by year, and be able to look back on his life with no regrets.

APPENDIX I

Managerial Growth Stage Checklist

The chart that follows is a checklist for you to verify your level as a manager and to clarify the problems you must now face and conquer. After reading this book, you may find it useful to use the checklist to examine yourself at regular intervals— for example, at the end of each fiscal year.

Please refer to the explanation following the checklist about how to use it.

Element evaluated / Stage of growth			Stage 0 Imperfect Maintenance Management	Stage 1 Maintenance Management
OCCUPATIONAL ASPECT		Precision of work	Errors and trouble still occur in every-day work; assistance of superiors is required to clean up the mess.	There are not too many errors or much trouble, but if there were, you could handle most of them alone.
		Ease of daily management	Work is mastering you instead of your mastering the work.	You're pretty much keeping up with your work, but you feel as though your hands are full with just that.
		Structural innovation	In some cases, work is not even finished according to the rules.	You can deal with standards problems and make minor improvements, but anything more than that would be very difficult for you.
HUMAN ASPECT		Trust	You do not have the full trust of your workers; there are still areas of mistrust.	No specific problem with trust, but you couldn't say you have the full trust of your staff.
		Motivation	The section is stagnated; there are still unresolved discontents.	The section isn't exactly stagnated, but then again it isn't exactly bursting with motivation.
		Development	You ruin your workers, or have a negative influence on them. Some talented young workers may even give up on you.	You're okay at developing new workers, but you haven't done so well with the development of the others.

Stage 2	Stage 3	Stage 4	Stage 5
Passive Structural Innovation	**Active Structural Innovation**		Combined Business Innovation
	Active Functional Innovation	Active Business Innovation	
There are very few errors and little trouble: you solve almost every problem by yourself.	You offer guidance to managers and key persons; you can maintain a trouble-free, error-free condition in your section.		You lead managers and head persons; you maintain a trouble-free, error-free section.
Daily work does not hinder maintenance management; you accept structural innovations from above.	Your staff does most of the daily work; you do not need to worry about it.	You carry out your managerial functions and can also effect structural innovations.	You lead, from top management down; you have plenty of leeway to effect innovations.
You can effect structural innovations with the guidance of your superiors.	You can influence others and effect a structural innovation upon a single function.	You can reconstruct and effect structural innovations on parts of processes on your own.	You can effect multiple structural innovations simultaneously on your own.
Your staff pretty well trusts you.	You have the full trust of all who work with you.		
You can change the atmosphere of your section but you cannot motivate every individual.	You can rework a stagnated section and make the whole staff feel completely involved.	You can rework a stagnated section and make the whole staff feel pletely involved.	You can completely change the head persons in your section and highly motivate every worker.
You have some development ability but you cannot change people. You are stumped by the "problem worker."	You can work changes in your staff, even in "problem workers." You are confident in your development ability.	You can change managers and key persons; the talents of workers you have developed are beginning to show.	You can change managers and head persons; you can develop workers for important positions and assignments.

HOW TO USE THE MANAGERIAL GROWTH STAGE CHECKLIST

1. Use the chart to determine your present stage of growth as a manager and to identify the problems you need to conquer.

2. Starting from each element in the "Element evaluated" column on the left side of the chart, read over to the right and place a check in the corner of the box that best describes your present level of ability. If the description in one box fits you fairly well but you are still not completely up to that level, check the box to its left. In your efforts to improve yourself, it will be to your advantage to judge on the strict side.

3. The column with the greatest number of boxes checked indicates your present level of managerial growth. The theme for your present self-improvement efforts is to bring every row up to that level. The theme for future efforts is to progress steadily to the right.

4. Newly appointed managers should pass through the stage of imperfect maintenance management in a maximum of one year.

5. Within three years, newly appointed managers will fall into one of the four major columns: imperfect maintenance management, maintenance management, passive structural innovation, or active structural innovation. Any newly appointed manager who attains the stage of active structural innovation within this time may be considered excellent.

6. General managers, assistant general managers, and section managers must be at the stage of active functional innovation. Operations managers and managers of a single division of a corporation must be at the stage of active business innovation; managers of head office operations and managers of multiple divisions of a corporation must be at the level of combined business innovation.

7. Your ability level for each element evaluated varies with the difficulty of your present position and your promotion history. Managers should recheck all their levels periodically—for example, at the end of each fiscal year—and reevaluate the directions for their future self-improvement efforts.

APPENDIX II

Manager Revolution Defined

The managers of the various organizations that make up contemporary Japanese society have serious problems in both ability and consciousness. These problems bear on many important social issues in Japan.

Why There Are So Many Problems in Noncorporate Organizations in Japan

Japan's noncorporate organizations, which include hospitals, schools, unions, and other groups, have encountered many problems in recent years.

These problems are the responsibility of the directors of the various organizations, but they cannot be solved simply by one director resigning and another taking his place. In today's gigantic organizations, the main supports of daily work activities are the general managers and division managers. If these managers themselves do not change, present conditions will continue indefinitely. The managers of hospitals, schools, unions, and other groups are at a far lower level than their corporate counterparts, for corporations have been working hard to develop the abilities of their managers since the 1950s. Whereas the corporate world has been working for more than twenty years to improve the human aspect of work, the top administrators of noncorporate organizations still show excessive concern for the occupational aspect, neglecting to develop the managers of their organizations properly.

The Crux of Japan's "Administrative Reform"

In the international arena, Japan can take pride in the vision, power, and sense of equilibrium of its bureaucratic structure. But there are still many problems with its "administrative reform" policy of cutting staff in governmental offices. Comparing Japan's bureaucracy—one form of social organization—with its corporate world sheds light on some factors that impede reform.

(1) Organizations that are too large, so that work cannot be handled smoothly.

In all organizations, each increase in size makes it more difficult for management to influence all the internal elements and more likely that members of the organization will become alienated.

The corporate world has combated this alienation by distributing authority to smaller and smaller operating sections, promoting small group activity, and thoroughly educating workers and managers at all levels. Managers of governmental offices, however, are still insufficiently aware of the physiological makeup of their organizations and have had no effective policy through their period of enormous growth.

(2) Top management awareness and term length.

In Japan the term of vice ministers and undersecretaries in governmental offices is usually two years or less. Cabinet members serve even shorter terms. In comparison, company presidents serve ten years or more, often retaining their positions for an entire generation.

The short tenure in governmental offices may be effective in ensuring that current problems are clearly understood and dealt with, but it is very weak where long-term internal policy is concerned. Since the effective functioning of an organization depends on the ability of its members, governmental offices must make a more consistent and long-term effort to raise consciousness, reform traditions, motivate workers, and develop their abilities.

Has the short term length been properly evaluated to determine its social utility? "Free-ride" managers can never effect necessary reforms.

(3) *The immaturity of labor-management relations, which is the foundation for reduced-staff operation.*

It is common knowledge throughout the corporate world that a relationship of mutual trust between labor and management is the basic premise for any reduced-staff operation.

Labor-management relations in postwar Japan's governmental offices were unlike those in the corporate world, where a new relationship of mutual trust was born from the aftermath of calamity. Labor-management relations in today's governmental offices are the cumulative result of long years of policymaking. The effects of this accumulation can be seen in the difference in character between the unions of public and private organizations.

Another factor in the problem is that politics tends to interfere in governmental labor-management relations. Top administrators are insufficiently aware of this, and there is no established structure to deal with high-level labor-management issues. Because of the frequent rotation of personnel, there is no opportunity for managers to develop specialized knowledge in this area.

The principal controlling factor in labor-management relations is the mutual trust between the workers and their superiors. Yet no steps have been taken to prevent worker alienation, and it is not clear how accurately the influence on worker morale of the "career/non-career" distinction has been evaluated. Management in governmental offices today is exactly as it was in the corporate world of the late 1940s and early 1950s. All human-related problems are left to those in lower management positions, and managers think that labor-management relations are none of their affair. This would seem to indicate a managerial retrogression.

(4) *Managers who place disproportionate emphasis on work quality and have no consciousness of cost.*

The days are long gone when the corporate world sacrificed economy and overemphasized work quality, but to the managers of governmental offices, staff reduction is still taboo. These managers are evaluated according to how big a budget they can get. Too many of them still think nothing can be done without great expenditures of money and labor. Some managers even believe that the fundamental concept of budgets is that they must always rise.

It is the mission of all social organizations to continue raising the quality of the work they do while lowering its cost at the same time. Managers and directors are the nucleus of this mission. The lack of cost-consciousness on the part of the managers and directors of governmental offices seems to have arisen from the general inadequacy of administrative structures and internal systems, and from the absence of proper leadership in a top-down organizational climate. What is worse, there is insufficient enthusiasm for manager development to reverse this trend, and an excessive attachment to formalities that is detrimental to the general awareness of the problems that must be corrected.

Japan's governmental organizations are strongly conservative, and their internal reforms during the cataclysmic last thirty years have been grossly inadequate. Managerial awareness is flawed with respect to cost and the human aspect of work.

Manager revolution is a core theme in administrative reform. The experience of the corporate world shows that staff reductions can never succeed without reforms in managerial awareness; even when they do seem successful, conditions regress in a short time and much priceless effort is tossed to the winds.

Taxes Are the Biggest Price Problem of All

The excessive burden imposed by rising federal and local taxes is something that all feel keenly. Inasmuch as they greatly reduce our disposable incomes, taxes are the biggest price problem of all. We are taxed according to fixed percentages, but as workers advance in rank they pay higher and higher amounts of tax. Any increase in the actual amount paid is a tax increase—even if the percentage remains the same. The government may disagree with this view, but no taxpayer will ever be convinced otherwise.

Suppose, just as an experiment, that we examine the factors that have reduced our present disposable incomes from last year's level. The factors include price rises in electricity, transportation and other necessities, and tax increases. Which of these puts the greatest burden on the individual consumer? Compared with the tax burden, the price rises to which industry is forced to resort are almost a pleasure to pay!

Taxes are the biggest price problem. It is therefore obvious that governmental offices must reduce their staffs, just as corporations must work hard to streamline their operations so they can absorb rising energy and labor costs. How can it be that the same nation that has achieved such efficiency in its corporations is incapable of doing the same in its government? The Japanese government's sense of equilibrium, in which we may all take pride, must now be applied to the problem of cost balancing.

Corporate Managers Beleaguered by Maintenance Management

The managers of Japan's corporations have been trained in an extremely competitive market that is unequaled anywhere else in the world, and high-quality organizational development puts them a step ahead of other organizations. Nevertheless, the managers of many large corporations are still beleaguered by routine work, and the number of managers who are ever actually able to make a lasting contribution to their organizations is extremely small. In this respect, corporate managers must learn from the examples set by their counterparts in central government offices and become capable of effecting policy reforms single-handedly.

The managers of large corporations lack the ability to change their workers. Their true duty as managers is to overcome this deficiency, endow their workers with new abilities over the years, change the ways their workers think and act, and devise ways of straightening out problem workers so they can find places for themselves.

The Developing Service Industries and Small Businesses

Workers in service industries already constitute a majority of the work force, but with the exception of a few established firms, the managers of these industries are inexperienced. Such problems are particularly common in the information industry.

Since the environment of the service industry is more permissive than that of the manufacturing industry, many companies have continued a policy of passing along every cost increase to the consumer. The managers of such businesses must perfect their maintenance management immediately.

The level of managerial skill in small businesses is generally low. The managers either do not know the basics of management or are incapable of applying what they know. The ability gap between the management of Japan's large corporations and that of her smaller corporations is an ever-present structural problem. The first step in closing this gap is for the managers to improve themselves.

Manager Revolution

In this book, I have discussed the serious problems in both consciousness and ability faced by managers of the organizations in every field of Japan's society today, and I have called earnestly for reforms to eliminate these problems.

In the tumultuous and unpredictable 1980s, we must let bygones be bygones. Everything hinges on how we face the future. Now is the time for the world's top administrators and directors to turn their attention to the development of managers. Now is the time for the managers themselves to come to grips with the problems they face. Now is the time for them to revolutionize their lives.

This is why I advocate manager revolution.

ABOUT THE AUTHOR

Yoshio Hatakeyama, one of Japan's most prominent management consultants, is the President of the Japan Management Association, the largest and most influential professional association of managers in Japan.

He is also the author of many Japanese business best sellers, one of which, *Managers Like This Should Resign!,* sold over one million copies. Other titles include *Why Do Companies Fail, Policy Making, Introduction to the Study of Business, People Who Develop Their Workers, It's Your Company—Protect It!, Employee Revolution,* and *Executive Revolution.*

Born in 1924 in Obihiro, Hokkaido, Hatakeyama graduated from the Ex-Paymaster's College and spent his early business career working in government offices, factories, and trading companies. In 1949, he joined the Japan Management Association as a management consultant and became a leader in management education. He provided surveys, advice, and training to public and private corporations. His professional specialties are in managerial surveys and management training.

Manager Revolution! is the first of Mr. Hatakeyama's books to be translated into English.

INDEX

A

Achievement
   motivating workers, role in, 123
Autonomy
   decision-making approach, 3-4

B

Beliefs
   manager, importance of, 109
Bodek, Norman, xvi
Bridgestone Tire, 88
Bureaucracy
   administrative reform, 168

C

Case method
   management education, of, 92
Change
   believing in it, 158
Classification
   problem, 75
Communication
   breakdown, 54
   contact, 54
   cycle, 52-53
   everyone's responsibility, 55
   negative reports, 53
   transmission content, 57
   speed, 55

Contact
   communication, 54
Cost
   quality control factor, 169-170
Cycle
   communications, 52-53
   management, 34

D

Decision making
   definition of, 80
   examining multiple alternatives, 85
   intuition-and-modification, 80
   methodology, 81-82, 86
   qualitative comparisons, 91
   quantitative comparisons, 91
   third party approach, 86-87
Desire
   personnel selection method, 34,
      39-40
Development
   changing way worker thinks, 131
   correcting negative traits, 131
   definition of, 131-132, 136
   enlarging worker skills, 131
   entrusting responsibility, 148
   experienced worker, of, 145-146
   human aspect of manager's job,
      22-23, 105

175

manager as example, 137
manager objectives, 133
managers, of, 150-154
new challenges, 136-137
patience and perseverance in, 140
strategy for, 131, 136-137, 141,
    148
workers, 131-132
Division of labor
group motivation through, 125-
    126
horizontal, 42, 126
predecessor's bequest, 9-10
successors and predecessors, 8
vertical, 42, 126

E

Education
management, 92
personnel selection method, 34,
    38-39
Entrustment
workers development strategy, 148
Evaluation
accomplishment as criterion for, 15
inadequacy of system for managers,
    14-15
managers' need to ignore, 13
managers, of, 6
problem-solving criteria, 77-79
self-evaluation for managers, 160-
    161
structural innovation, 102
Experience
personnel selection method, 34,
    36-37

F

Flexible manufacturing system, xv
Fukuda, Ryuji
    Managerial Engineering, xv

G

General manager
developing managers, role in, 153
structural innovation, role in, 154
go, 120

Government
labor-management relations in
    Japan, 14, 169
Group motivation
dividing work, 125-126
setting attractive objectives, 123-
    124

H

Hana-tsubaki kai (Camellia-flower
    Club), 65
Harvard Business School, 92
Health
managers, of, 161
Horizontal division of responsibilities,
    126
Human ability
personnel selection method, 34,
    35-36
potential, 45-46
realized, 45
Human relations
management responsibility for, 22
Humility
manager, importance of, 22, 160

I

Imagination
structural innovation, role in, 68
Industrial study missions
Japan, xvi
Innovation, structural
see Structural innovation
Investigation
problem identification, 71-72
Ishibashi, Seijiro, 88

J

Japan
ability gap in management of cor-
    porations, 172
administrative reform, 168
industrial study missions to, xvi
labor-management relations, 169
manager revolution, 170
noncorporate organizations, 167
service industries, 171

taxes as price problem, 170
techniques of management, 89-90
Japan Management Association, xvi,
173

K

K J method of problem solving, 76, 90
Kanban, xv, 90
Kawakita, Jiro
K J method of problem solving, 76
Knowledge
structural innovation, role in, 68

L

Labor-management relations
Japan, 169

M

MDP *see* Management Development
Program
Maintenance management
beleaguers managers, 171
definition of, 18, 29, 46
occupational aspect of manager's
job, 18
Management
cycle, 34
day-to-day operations, 33
definition of, 26
development element, 22
education for, 92
human aspect of, 20, 25, 105
levels of, 23
MDP technique, 135
maintenance element, 18
motivation element, 22
occupational aspect of, 18-20, 25
standards of work quantity, 32-33
structural innovation element, 18
techniques used in Japan, 89-90
trust element, 22
Management consultant, 93
Management Development Program
American management technique,
135
Managerial reform
reason for, xvii

Manager revolution
definition of, 167
need for, 172
theme in Japan's administrative
reform, 170
Managers
ability to influence higher management, 109
acting on beliefs, 13
autonomy of decision making, 3-4
character, 106-108
definition of, 1, 7, 15-16
development of, 151-153
difficulties to be overcome, 66-67
division of responsibilities, 8
enthusiasm for work, 106
evaluation by achievement, 13, 15,
56
example for worker development,
137
fairness, 108
friends and advisors, 159
functions of, 4-5
getting away from role as judge, 128
growth stage checklist
description, 163-66
health, 161
interdepartment obstacles, 49
Japan's ability gap, 171-172
maintenance management, 171
making a lasting contribution, 7
need to revolutionize self, 158
new position factors to consider, 31
new position objectives, 32
"one position, one accomplishment," 7, 10, 16
persuasive power, 93
qualities affecting worker trust,
107-108
responsibility for worker support,
46, 51, 109-110
self-awareness, 2-3
self-development, 30, 158-159
selfishness, 106
small group activity, role in, 127
strong will, 95
tasks of new manager, 8, 11-12

unity of decision making, 3-4
views and beliefs, importance of,
    109
Measurement
  method of making work interesting,
    119-120
Mobilization
  colleagues, of, 5
  superiors, of, 5
  those outside the organization, of, 5
Motivation
  creating a stimulating work envi-
    ronment, 111
  definition of, 111-112
  direct forms of, 111
  good managerial habits needed, 114
  group, 123
  group approach strategy, 117
  human aspect of manager's job, 22,
    105
  indirect forms of, 111
  individual approach strategy, 117-
    118
  prerequisites for, 114-115
  recognizing individual strengths,
    118-119
  small group activity, 126-127
  worker trust as prerequisite, 114

O

Organizations
  intra-department obstacles, 49
  manager autonomy and unity, 3-4
  manager contribution as permanent
    asset, 8
  negative factors within, 117
  noncorporate, problems of, 167
  predecessors bequests to new mana-
    gers, 9-10
  small group activity, 127
  social function of, 17, 26
Ouchi, William
  Theory Z, xv

P

Participative management, xv

Personality
  personnel selection method, 34, 38
Personnel selection
  ability, by, 35
  comprehensive analysis, need for,
    41
  decision strategy, 41
  desire, by, 39-40
  education, by, 38-39
  experience, by, 36-37
  personality, by, 38
  seniority, by, 34-35
Persuasion
  analyzing other party, 97
  convincing higher management, 98
  elements of, 71, 93-95
  priming others and setting the scene
    for change, 98-100.
  strong will needed, 95
  structural innovation aspect, 69, 93
  work environment improvement,
    49
Planning
  daily management, 33-34
  structural innovation, 100
Position, new
  daily management routines, 33-34
  objectives, 32
  opportunity for self-development,
    30
  points for manager to consider, 31
  putting internal system in order,
    32-33
Problem-solving
  costs of, 77
  current vs. future problems, 78
  timing, 78
  work vs. human problems, 79
Problems
  classification of, 74
  identification of, 73
  standards for evaluation of, 76
Public agencies
  managerial weaknesses, xviii
Pursuit of targets
  method of making work interesting,
    120-121

Q

Quality control
  cost-consciousness needed, 169-170
Quality control circles, xv, 127

R

Reform
  administrative reform in Japan, 168
  factors that impede, 168-169
  structural innovation, through, 102
Remedial education
  development strategy for experienced workers, 145

S

Schonberger, Richard
  Japanese Manufacturing Techniques, xv
Self-awareness
  managers, of, 2-3
Self-development
  managers, of, 30
Self-evaluation
  managers, of, 160
Seniority
  personnel selection methods, 34, 35-36
Service industries
  managerial skill in, 171
Shingo, Shigeo
  Study of the Toyota Production System, xv
Shiseido, 65
Small group activity
  definition of, 126
  manager's role in, 127
Standards
  problem evaluation, 76
  work quantity, 32-33
Structural innovation
  barriers to, 61, 66-67
  change inside the organization, 60
  change outside the organization, 60
  cost increases, 61
  decision making, 71, 80
  definition of, 18, 29, 59

education for, 101
evaluation measures, 102
forms of, 59-60
general manager responsibilities, 154
growth stages of manager's job, 18-20
implementation planning, 100
insufficient knowledge, 68
investigation stage, 71
lack of imagination, 67-68
lack of persuasive power, 69
modeling, 101
planning, 100
prerequisites of, 63-65
setting the scene for change, 98-99
strategy for effecting, 70-71
types of, 62
winning agreement of higher management, 98
Support
  manager's responsibility for backing up workers, 109-110

T

Taxation
  biggest price problem in Japan, 170
Taylor system, 89
Teamwork
  work motivation, importance in, 112
Time management
  structural innovation, importance in, 69
Timing
  balancing time and entrustment, 149
Training
  experienced workers, 147
  managers, 150-151
  new workers, 143-144
Trust
  human aspect of manager's job, element in, 22, 105
  labor-management relations, factor in, 169
  manager's persuasive power, element in, 94

U-V

Unity
  manager's approach to decision
    making, 3-4
Vertical division of responsibilities,
  126

W

Work
  balance between work and workers,
    24
  development, as, 139
  educational medium, as, 139
  independence, 9
  making it interesting, 118-
    119
Work environment
  definition of, 42
  division of responsibilities, 42-43,
    125
  preconditions for, 47-48
  reform of, 129
  strategy for building, 45-46
  worker motivation, importance in,
    111
Workers
  balance between work and workers,
    24
  bringing out the will to work, 112
  deficiencies supplemented by man-
    ager, 50-51
  development by entrusting, 148
  development by manager example,
    137

  discontented with position, 122
  experienced, defeatism of, 147
  experienced, development of, 145-
    146
  experienced, overdependent on
    manager, 147
  experienced, problems needing
    correction, 147
  insufficient ability, 50
  joy of achievement, 123
  management development of, 22-
    23, 45-46, 131
  manager's responsibility for, 20
  motivation of, 22, 111, 127
  new challenges for, 136-137
  new, learning how to enjoy work,
    142
  new, show and tell method, 145
  patience and perseverance of man-
    ager, 140-141
  potential, 134
  problem workers, 121-123
  room for growth, 44
  support of managers, 46, 51, 109-
    110
  tools, as, 24
  trust of management, 22, 106
World War II, 65, 142

Y-Z

Yamamoto, Isoroku, Admiral, 142
Zero-defects, 127

BOOKS AVAILABLE FROM PRODUCTIVITY PRESS

Productivity Press publishes and distributes materials on productivity, quality improvement, and employee involvement for business and industry, academia, and the general market. Many products are direct source materials from Japan that have been translated into English for the first time and are available exclusively from Productivity. Supplemental services include conferences, seminars, in-house training programs, and industrial study missions. Send for free book catalog.

The Improvement Book
Creating the Problem-Free Workplace

by Tomoo Sugiyama

A practical guide to setting up a participatory problem- solving system in the workplace. This book provides clear direction for starting a problem-free engineering program, a full introduction to basic concepts of industrial housekeeping (known in Japan as 5S), two chapters of examples that can be used in small group training activities, and a workbook for individual use. Informal, using many anecdotes and examples, this book provides a proven fundamental approach to problem solving for any industrial setting.
ISBN 0-915299-47-X / 320 pages / $49.95 / Order code IB-BK

The Idea Book
Improvement Through Total Employee Involvement

edited by the Japan Human Relations Association

What would your company be like if each employee — from line workers to engineers to sales people — gave 100 ideas every year for improving the company? This handbook of Japanese-style suggestion systems (called "teian"), will help your company develop its own vital improvement system by getting all employees involved. Train workers how to write improvement proposals, help supervisors promote participation, and put creative problem solving to work in your company. Designed as a self-trainer and study group tool, the book is heavily illustrated and includes hundreds of examples.
ISBN 0-915299-22-4 / 232 pages / $49.95 / Order code IDEA-BK

Productivity Press, Inc., Dept. BK, P.O. Box 3007, Cambridge, MA 02140 1-800-274-9911

JIT Factory Revolution
Hiroyuki Hirano/JIT Management Library

Here at last is the first-ever encyclopedic picture book of JIT. Using 240 pages of photos, cartoons, and diagrams, this unprecedented behind-the-scenes look at actual production and assembly plants shows you exactly how JIT looks and functions. It shows you how to set up each area of a JIT plant and provides hundreds of useful ideas you can implement. If you've made the crucial decision to run production using JIT and want to show your employees what it's all about, this book is a must. The photographs, from various Japanese production and assembly plants, provide vivid depictions of what work is like in a JIT environment. And the text, simple and easy to read, makes all the essentials crystal clear.
ISBN 0-915299-44-5 / 240 pages / illustrated / $49.95 / Order code JITFAC-BK

Management for Quality Improvement
The 7 New QC Tools
edited by Shigeru Mizuno

Building on the traditional seven QC tools, these new tools were developed specifically for managers. They help in planning, troubleshooting, and communicating with maximum effectiveness at every stage of a quality improvement program. Just recently made available in the U.S., they are certain to advance quality improvement efforts for anyone involved in project management, quality assurance, MIS, or TQC.
ISBN 0-915299-29-1 / 318 pages / $59.95 / Order code 7QC-BK

Inside Corporate Japan
The Art of Fumble-Free Management
by David J. Lu

A major advance in the effort to increase our understanding of Japan, this book shows *why* Japanese businesses are run as they are — and how American companies can put this knowledge to good use. Lu has spent many years in Japan, personally knows many top leaders in industry and government, and writes with a unique bicultural perspective. His very readable book is full of anecdotes, case studies, interviews, and careful scholarship. He paints a well-rounded picture of the underlying dynamics of successful Japanese companies. *Inside Corporate Japan* is a timely and invaluable addition to your library.
ISBN 0-915299-16-X / 278 pages / $24.95 / Order code ICJ-BK

Workplace Management

Taiichi Ohno

An in-depth view of how one of this century's leading industrial thinkers approaches problem solving and continuous improvement. Gleaned from Ohno's forty years of experimentation and innovation at Toyota Motor Co., where he created JIT, this book explains the concepts Ohno considers most important to successful management, with an emphasis on quality.

ISBN 0-915299-19-4 / 165 pages / $34.95 / Order code WPM-BK

TO ORDER: Write, phone, or fax Productivity Press, Dept. BK, P.O. Box 3007, Cambridge, MA 02140, phone 1-800-274-9911, fax 617-868-3524. Send check or charge to your credit card (American Express, Visa, MasterCard accepted).

U.S. ORDERS: Add $4 shipping for first book, $2 each additional. CT residents add 7.5% and MA residents 5% sales tax.

FOREIGN ORDERS: Payment must be made in U.S. dollars (checks must be drawn on U.S. banks). For Canadian orders, add $10 shipping for first book, $2 each additional. For orders to other countries write, phone, or fax for quote and indicate shipping method desired.

NOTE: Prices subject to change without notice.

Productivity Press, Inc., Dept. BK, P.O. Box 3007, Cambridge, MA 02140 1-800-274-9911

BOOKS AVAILABLE FROM PRODUCTIVITY PRESS

Buehler, Vernon M. and Y.K. Shetty (eds.). **Competing Through Productivity and Quality**
ISBN 0-915299-43-7 / 1989 / 576 pages / $39.95 / order code COMP

Christopher, William F. **Productivity Measurement Handbook**
ISBN 0-915299-05-4 / 1985 / 680 pages / $137.95 / order code PMH

Ford, Henry. **Today and Tomorrow**
ISBN 0-915299-36-4 / 1988 / 286 pages / $24.95 / order code FORD

Fukuda, Ryuji. **Managerial Engineering: Techniques for Improving Quality and Productivity in the Workplace**
ISBN 0-915299-09-7 / 1984 / 206 pages / $34.95 / order code ME

Hatakeyama, Yoshio. **Manager Revolution! A Guide to Survival in Today's Changing Workplace**
ISBN 0-915299-10-0 / 1985 / 208 pages / $24.95 / order code MREV

Hirano, Hiroyuki. **JIT Factory Revolution: A Pictorial Guide to Factory Design of the Future**
ISBN 0-915299-44-5 / 1989 / 218 pages / $49.95 / order code JITFAC

Japan Human Relations Association (ed.). **The Idea Book: Improvement Through TEI (Total Employee Involvement)**
ISBN 0-915299-22-4 / 1988 / 232 pages / $49.95 / order code IDEA

Japan Management Association (ed.). **Kanban and Just-In-Time at Toyota: Begins at the Workplace** (Revised Ed.), Translated by David J. Lu
ISBN 0-915299-48-8 / 1989 / 224 pages / $34.95 / order code KAN

Japan Management Association and Constance E. Dyer. **The Canon Production System: Creative Involvement of the Total Workforce**
ISBN 0-915299-06-2 / 1987 / 251 pages / $36.95 / order code CAN

Karatsu, Hajime. **Tough Words For American Industry**
ISBN 0-915299-25-9 / 1988 / 178 pages / $24.95 / order code TOUGH

Karatsu, Hajime. **TQC Wisdom of Japan: Managing for Total Quality Control**, Translated by David J. Lu
ISBN 0-915299-18-6 / 1988 / 136 pages / $34.95 / order code WISD

Lu, David J. **Inside Corporate Japan: The Art of Fumble-Free Management**
ISBN 0-915299-16-X / 1987 / 278 pages / $24.95 / order code ICJ

Mizuno, Shigeru (ed.). **Management for Quality Improvement: The 7 New QC Tools**
ISBN 0-915299-29-1 / 1988 / 318 pages / $59.95 / order code 7QC

Monden, Yashuhiro and Sakurai, Michiharu. **Japanese Management Accounting: A World Class Approach to Profit Management**
ISBN 0-915299-50-X / 1989 / 512 pages / $49.95 / order code JMACT

Nakajima, Seiichi. **Introduction to TPM: Total Productive Maintenance**
ISBN 0-915299-23-2 / 1988 / 149 pages / $39.95 / order code ITPM

Nakajima, Seiichi. **TPM Development Program: Implementing Total Productive Maintenance**
ISBN 0-915299-37-2 / 1989 / 528 pages / $85.00 / order code DTPM

Productivity Press, Inc., Dept. BK, P.O. Box 3007, Cambridge, MA 02140 1-800-274-9911

Nikkan Kogyo Shimbun, Ltd./Factory Magazine (ed.). **Poka-yoke: Improving Product Quality by Preventing Defects**
ISBN 0-915299-31-3 / 1989 / 288 pages / $59.95 / order code IPOKA

Ohno, Taiichi. **Toyota Production System: Beyond Large-Scale Production**
ISBN 0-915299-14-3 / 1988 / 163 pages / $39.95 / order code OTPS

Ohno, Taiichi. **Workplace Management**
ISBN 0-915299-19-4 / 1988 / 165 pages / $34.95 / order code WPM

Ohno, Taiichi and Setsuo Mito. **Just-In-Time for Today and Tomorrow**
ISBN 0-915299-20-8 / 1988 / 208 pages / $34.95 / order code OMJIT

Psarouthakis, John. **Better Makes Us Best**
ISBN 0-915299-56-9 / 1989 / 112 pages / $16.95 / order code BMUB

Shingo, Shigeo. **Non-Stock Production: The Shingo System for Continuous Improvement**
ISBN 0-915299-30-5 / 1988 / 480 pages / $75.00 / order code NON

Shingo, Shigeo. **A Revolution In Manufacturing: The SMED System**, Translated by Andrew P. Dillon
ISBN 0-915299-03-8 / 1985 / 383 pages / $65.00 / order code SMED

Shingo, Shigeo. **The Sayings of Shigeo Shingo: Key Strategies for Plant Improvement**, Translated by Andrew P. Dillon
ISBN 0-915299-15-1 / 1987 / 208 pages / $36.95 / order code SAY

Shingo, Shigeo. **A Study of the Toyota Production System from an Industrial Engineering Viewpoint** (Revised Ed.),
ISBN 0-915299-17-8 / 1989 / 352 pages / $39.95 / order code STREV

Shingo, Shigeo. **Zero Quality Control: Source Inspection and the Poka-yoke System**, Translated by Andrew P. Dillon
ISBN 0-915299-07-0 / 1986 / 328 pages / $65.00 / order code ZQC

Shinohara, Isao (ed.). **New Production System: JIT Crossing Industry Boundaries**
ISBN 0-915299-21-6 / 1988 / 224 pages / $34.95 / order code NPS

Sugiyama, Tomō. **The Improvement Book: Creating the Problem-free Workplace**
ISBN 0-915299-47-X / 1989 / 320 pages / $49.95 / order code IB

Tateisi, Kazuma. **The Eternal Venture Spirit: An Executive's Practical Philosophy**
ISBN 0-915299-55-0 / 1989 / 208 pages / $19.95 / order code EVS

Productivity Press, Inc., Dept. BK, P.O. Box 3007, Cambridge, MA 02140 1-800-274-9911

AUDIO-VISUAL PROGRAMS

Japan Management Association. **Total Productive Maintenance: Maximizing Productivity and Quality**
ISBN 0-915299-46-1 / 167 slides / 1989 / $749.00 / order code STPM
ISBN 0-915299-49-6 / 2 videos / 1989 / $749.00 / order code VTPM

Shingo, Shigeo. **The SMED System**, Translated by Andrew P. Dillon
ISBN 0-915299-11-9 / 181 slides / 1986 / $749.00 / order code S5
ISBN 0-915299-27-5 / 2 videos / 1987 / $749.00 / order code V5

Shingo, Shigeo. **The Poka-yoke System**, Translated by Andrew P. Dillon
ISBN 0-915299-13-5 / 235 slides / 1987 / $749.00 / order code S6
ISBN 0-915299-28-3 / 2 videos / 1987 / $749.00 / order code V6

TO ORDER: Write, phone, or fax Productivity Press, Dept. BK, P.O. Box 3007, Cambridge, MA 02140, phone 1-800-274-9911, fax 617-868- 3524. Send check or charge to your credit card (American Express, Visa, MasterCard accepted).

U.S. ORDERS: Add $4 shipping for first book, $2 each additional. CT residents add 7.5% and MA residents 5% sales tax.

FOREIGN ORDERS: Payment must be made in U.S. dollars (checks must be drawn on U.S. banks). For Canadian orders, add $10 shipping for first book, $2 each additional. For orders to other countries write, phone, or fax for quote and indicate shipping method desired.

NOTE: Prices subject to change without notice.